SECOND EDITION

GREEK ^{THE}& LATIN

ROOTS OF ENGLISH

SECOND EDITION

GREEK ᵀᴴᴱ & LATIN
ROOTS OF ENGLISH

TAMARA M. GREEN

HUNTER COLLEGE OF THE CITY UNIVERSITY OF NEW YORK

ARDSLEY HOUSE, PUBLISHERS, INC. NEW YORK

For Claireve,
whose bright idea this was

Address orders and editorial
correspondence to:
Ardsley House, Publishers, Inc.
320 Central Park West
New York, NY 10025

ISBN: 1-880157-09-8

Printed in the United States of America

10 9 8 7 6 5 4 3 2

CONTENTS

PREFACE

"Language is a city to the building of which every human being brought a stone." Emerson's words are a recognition that the development of our own language and the way in which we use it have been, in large measure, historically and culturally determined.

As a result of both the accidents of history and the great esteem in which ancient Greco-Roman civilization has been held in the Western tradition, over 60% of all English words have Greek or Latin roots; in the vocabulary of the sciences and technology, the figure rises to over 90%. Thus, through the study of the Greek and Latin roots of English, students not only can expand their knowledge of English vocabulary, but, just as importantly, be made aware of the functions and modes of expression in a variety of languages.

The approach of this text is thematic: vocabulary is organized into various topics, including politics and government, medicine and the sciences, psychology, literature, and religion. Unlike those textbooks that treat Latin and Greek roots separately, these lessons present the two vocabularies as an organic whole. Thus, the emphasis is placed on language and the way in which it develops and changes, rather than on single words, or even groups of words. The exercises at the end of each section are cumulative, reinforcing both vocabulary already learned and analytical skills developed in previous lessons.

In addition to teaching vocabulary skills, the text has another, perhaps more subtle, aim. It is hoped that through the study of the Greek and Latin roots of English, students will begin to recognize the pleasures (and pitfalls) of language study.

The original development of the materials for this text was made possible by a grant to Hunter College from the National Endowment for the Humanities.

NEW MATERIAL IN THE SECOND EDITION

The Second Edition has retained the organization and thematic approach of the earlier edition. Because of the great interest shown by science students, the new edition now contains three chapters dealing with terminology in medicine, mathematics, and the various branches of the natural sciences. In addition, there are new chapters treating the social sciences, education, and classical influences on the arts and on society in general. New materials have also been added in many of the chapters that appeared in the original edition. Many new exercises have been added in most chapters.

HOW TO USE THIS TEXT

An English word followed by Greek in parentheses indicates that the word is Greek.

In the vocabulary, both the nominative and genitive cases are given for all Latin nouns and adjectives. The principal parts of Latin verbs are also given.

Because most words derived from Greek are learned borrowings, the genitive case of a noun or adjective is rarely cited, unless the compound form of the word is derived from that case.

Vocabulary words are occasionally repeated in different lessons when necessary.

SYMBOLS USED

Symbol	Meaning
=	English meaning
> > >	from which is derived

INSTRUCTOR'S MANUAL

An Instructor's Manual is available to adopters of this text. It contains:

- Quizzes on each chapter or group of chapters (two versions in most cases)

- Two final examinations
- Answers to all quizzes and final examinations
- Answers to all the exercises in the text.

PHOTOGRAPHS

All photographs in the book are from the author's private collection.

SECOND EDITION

GREEK ^{THE}& LATIN

ROOTS OF ENGLISH

Riders on horseback. Corinthian crater (570 B.C.)

When you cook a crane, make sure that the head does not touch the water, but is outside it. When it has been cooked, wrap it in a warm cloth and pull its head.

APICIUS (1ST CENTURY A.D. ROMAN GOURMET),
About Cooking

A POLYGLOT STEW

(OR "FOOD FOR THOUGHT")

If, in fact, we are what we eat, the American people are the most cosmopolitan nation in the world. Just as English is a mixture of Germanic, Latin, and Greek roots with a heavy seasoning of the Romance Languages, with just a dash of Indian, African, and Caribbean, so does our diet reflect the various linguistic elements that go into the melting pot of American cuisine.

The Normans conquered England in A.D. 1066 and introduced, via French, Latin-based names for various foods; nevertheless, although English tastes and vocabulary were about to be expanded, the Germanic component of the English menu did not disappear. For example, Middle English *mete* made peace with the Old French *boef*, thus allowing us to enjoy both meat and beef, while the Germanic-based *chiken* nested quite comfortably with the French *poulet*. And if the English seemed to have lost their *appetite* after the Norman conquest, the French tempted their *palates* with the introduction of such foods as *salmon*, *rice*, and *carrots*. French *pain*, however, never replaced Old English *bread*. Perhaps they found that too painful to contemplate.

PLANNING DINNER

Well, what shall we have for dinner? We can eat geographically, as it were, starting off with some Latin-based *wine*, Gaelic *whiskey*, or Russian *vodka*. The German cities of *Hamburg* and *Frankfort* give us two staples of the American diet, whose flavor we enhance by adding Chinese *ketchup*, French *mustard*, or a Dutch *pickle*. Or would you prefer Italian *pasta*: *linguini*, perhaps, or *spaghetti*, topped with the most famous product of *Parma*, Italy?

Of course, a well-balanced meal needs a French *salad* filled with native and imported *vegetables*: the Indians of North and South America can provide *squash*, *tomatoes*, *potatoes*, and *avocados*, while the Arabs will serve *spinach*. We can add a classical touch with *onions*, *lettuce*, and *peas*: the lowly *radish* also has a Latin root.

This well-balanced meal can be ended with some *fruit* for dessert: an *orange* from Persia, or a *banana* from West Africa, or a much-traveled *apricot*, which passed from Latin into Arabic and then returned into Portuguese. If our taste buds crave something sweeter, however, what could be more American than *apple pie*? Or would you prefer some Teutonic *cake* or a *pretzel*, or perhaps a Dutch *cookie*? You can wash it all down with some *coffee* from Turkey or all the *tea* in China.

Vocabulary

meat = from Old English *mete*
beef = from Old French *boef* (from Latin bos, bovis = cow)
  cf. Modern French boeuf
chicken = from Germanic *chiken*, cf. Old English *cicen*
poultry = from Middle French *poulet* (from Latin *pullus* = young of any animal)
  cf. Spanish and Italian *pollo*
appetite = from Latin verb *appeto* = to seek, desire
palate = from Latin *palatum* = roof of the mouth
salmon = from French *saumon* (from Latin *salmo, salmonis* = salmon)
rice = from Old French *ris*, from Italian *riso* (from Greek *oryzon*)
carrot = from French *carotte*, from Latin *carota* (from Greek *karoton*)
bread = from Old English *bread*
  cf. German *brot*
  but Latin *panis* = bread > > >
    French *pain*
    Italian *pane*
    Spanish *pan*
wine = from Latin *vinum* > > >
    French *vin*
    Italian and Spanish *vino*
whiskey = from Gaelic *usquebaugh* ("the water of life")
vodka = from Russian *voda* (water)

pasta = from Latin *pasta* (dough), from Greek *pastos* = sprinkled. Originally, pasta was a kind of porridge sprinkled with salt.

  linguini = from Latin *lingua* (tongue)

  spaghetti = from Italian *spago* (cord, rope)

salad = from French *salade* (Latin *salata* = salted)

  cf. Latin *sal* (salt)

vegetable = from Latin verb *vegeo* (grow)

squash = from Narragansett American Indian *askutasquash* (thing eaten green)

tomato = from Spanish *tomate* (from Aztec *tomatl*)

potato = from Spanish *patata* (from West Indian *batata*)

avocado = from Spanish *aguacate* (from Nahuatl Indian *ahuacatl* = testicle)

spinach = from Old Spanish *espinaca* (from Arabic *isfanakh*)

radish = from Old English *raedic* (from Latin *radix* = root)

fruit = from Latin verb *fruor* = enjoy

apricot = the original form of the word in English was apricock, from Portuguese *albricoque*, which, in turn, came from the Arabic *al birquq*. The Arabic word, however, had been, in turn, a transliteration of a Latin adjective, *praecoquum* (early ripening), a term that could be applied to any fruit.

apple = from Old English *aeppel*

  cf. German *apfel*

pie = from Middle English *pie* (shallow pit)

  from Old French *puis* (from Latin *puleus* = well)

cake = from Middle English *kake*

  cf. Icelandic *kaka*

    German *kuchen*

    Dutch *coek*. Cookie is a diminutive form of *coek*.

pretzel = from German *bretzel* (from Latin *bracellus* = bracelet)

coffee = from Turkish *kahve* (from Arabic *qahwah*)

tea = from Chinese *t'e* (dialect); the more common word for tea in Chinese is the Mandarin *ch'a*.

Corinth

And the whole earth was of one language and of one speech... And they said, "Come let us build us a city, and a tower, with its top in heaven, and let us make us a name; lest we be scattered abroad upon the face of the whole earth." And the Lord came down to see the city and the tower, which the children of men built. And the Lord said, "Behold, they are one people, and they have all one language; and this is what they begin to do; and now nothing will be withholden from them, which they purpose to do. Come let us go down, and there confound their language, that they may not understand one another's speech." So the Lord scattered them abroad from thence upon the face of the earth; and they left off to build the city. Therefore was the name of it called Babel, because the Lord did there confound the language of all the earth.

Genesis, xi:1–9
(JEWISH PUBLICATION SOCIETY)

LANGUAGE FAMILIES

LANGUAGE AND HISTORY

Language is a human activity, and like all human activities, it seems to have an infinite variability. Nevertheless, within that variability, patterns and relationships can be discovered. The languages of the world (and the experts estimate that the number of languages ranges from 2,900 to nearly 10,000) are divided into various families, the members of which are considered by linguists to be related because of similarities in structure, grammar, and vocabulary. The major families, or trees, of human languages are the following:

1. Indo-European
2. Afro-Asiatic (formerly known as Semitic-Hamitic: Arabic, Hebrew, Amharic, Coptic)
3. Sino-Tibetan (Chinese, Tibetan, Thai, Burmese)
4. Japanese and Korean
5. Uralic-Altaic (Finnish, Estonian, Hungarian, Turkish, Mongol)
6. Caucasian (spoken in the Caucasus Mountains of Georgia, Armenia, and Azerbaijan)
7. Dravidian (spoken in Southern India)
8. Malayo-Polynesian (the languages of the South Pacific and Indian Ocean)
9. Austroasiatic (Cambodian, Vietnamese)

10. African*
11. North and South American Indian*
12. the orphans: single languages that seem to bear no connection with any other: e.g., Ainu, which is spoken by the aboriginal inhabitants of Japan, or Basque, the language of the inhabitants of the Pyrenees region of Spain and France.

THE BRANCHES OF THE INDO-EUROPEAN TREE

The largest and most widely diffused of these language families is Indo-European. Like everything else in the realm of human activity, language is subject to change, and many languages have disappeared or evolved into other languages over the centuries. For example, Latin is no longer spoken, but it survives through its direct descendants, Italian, French, and Spanish. Other ancient languages, however, have disappeared without a trace because they were not written down.

Linguists have classified the surviving branches of the Indo-European tree as follows:

1. *Indian*	2. *Iranian*	3. *Hellenic*	4. *Italic*
Sanskrit†	Avestan†	Ancient Greek†	Latin†
Hindi	Old Persian†	Byzantine Greek†	Italian
Bengali	Modern Persian	Modern Greek	French
Punjabi	Pashto	Macedonian‡	Spanish
Mahrati	Kurdish	Yavanic	Portuguese
Urdu	Beluchi		Romanian
Sinhalese			
Romany			

5. *Germanic (Teutonic)*	6. *Celtic*	7. *Slavonic*
Gothic†	Galatian†	Great Russian
Middle High German†	Gaulish†	Belorussian
Modern German	Celtiberian†	Ukrainian

---

*Strictly speaking, these are divisions that are based on geographic proximity, rather than on the usual rules of linguistic classification, because there is a great deal of disagreement about their relationship to one another. There are estimated to be over 700 African and 1200 American Indian languages.

†No longer spoken.

‡Macedonian shows elements of both Slavic and Greek.

Germanic	*Celtic*	*Slavonic*
Yiddish	Brittonic†	Sorbian
Dutch	Cornish	Kashubian
Flemish	Welsh	Polish
Frisian	Breton	Slovene
Old English (Anglo-Saxon)†	Gaelic	Slovak
Middle English†	(a) Irish	Czech
Modern English	(b) Scottish	Serbo-Croatian
Afrikaans	(c) Manx	Bulgarian
Scandinavian		Macedonian‡
(a) Norwegian		
(b) Icelandic		
(c) Swedish		
(d) Danish		
(e) Faroese		

8. *Baltic*	9. *Illyrian*	10. *Thraco-Phrygian*
Lithuanian	Albanian	Thracian†
Latvian		Phrygian†
		Armenian

AN OUTLINE OF THE HISTORY OF THE ENGLISH LANGUAGE

Although English is classified as belonging to the Germanic branch of the Indo-European tree because of its historical origins and development, its vocabulary has been strongly influenced, through the accidents of history and politics, by other Indo-European languages, most notably Latin and its offshoots and, to a lesser extent, Greek. What follows is a brief outline of the historical and cultural events that influenced the development of the English language.

The Roman Occupation of Britain: first century A.D.–A.D. 410
1. Celtic languages (also Indo-European)
2. Introduction of Latin, the language of Roman conquest and commerce
3. Withdrawal of the Roman army: 410

Old English: A.D. 450–A.D. 1150
1. Invasion of the Germanic tribes (Angles, Saxons, Jutes): 449

2. Conversion of the Anglo-Saxons to Christianity: 597
   Reintroduction of Latin *via* the Church
3. Viking (Danish) raids on Britain: 8th–9th centuries
4. *Beowulf* (Anglo-Saxon): 8th–9th centuries
5. The Norman Conquest: 1066
   Reintroduction of Latin-based vocabulary *via* French

Middle English: A.D. 1150–A.D. 1500
1. The Anglo-French connection
2. Changes in vocabulary: loss of many Old English (Germanic) words; addition of thousands of words from French and Latin
3. Changes in grammar: loss of inflection
4. The development of a vernacular literature:
   Chaucer: *Canterbury Tales*
   Langland: *Piers Plowman*
5. First translation of Bible from Latin into English, perhaps by John Wycliffe
6. Introduction of the printing press into England by William Caxton (1476)

Modern English: A.D. 1500–present
1. Decline of Latin as a common European language of discourse and the rise of vernacular languages
2. Translations of classical Greek and Latin texts (Renaissance)
3. Shakespeare (1564–1616)
4. Standardization of spelling (*orthography*) and enrichment of vocabulary (16th–17th centuries)
5. Dr. Samuel Johnson: *A Dictionary of the English Language* (1755)
6. Grammarians and rhetoricians: the formation of rules (18th century)
7. The development of the scientific study of comparative, historical, and structural linguistics (18th century)
8. The influence of British and American colonialism and Empire (19th–20th centuries)

THE DEVELOPMENT OF AMERICAN ENGLISH

England and America are two countries separated by the same language.
George Bernard Shaw

From the settlement of Jamestown to the end of the colonial period: 1607–1790

1. The establishment of the forms and patterns of American English, as distinct from British English

The period of Westward expansion: 1790–1860
1. Immigration from Western Europe and Ireland
2. Noah Webster: *An American Dictionary of the English Language* (1828)
3. Mobility of the population; settlement of the Far West

The period since the Civil War: 1861 to the present
1. Emancipation of the slaves (1863)
2. Immigration from Eastern and Southern Europe (1880–1920)
3. Immigration from the Caribbean and South America (1945–present)
4. Immigration from Asia and the Pacific Rim (1975–present)
5. Uniformity of language vs. regionalism: the influence of radio, television, and the movies

SOME USEFUL TERMS

etymology: the study of the history of a particular word; the derivation or origin of a word

linguistics: the science of language, including the history, formation, and structures of languages

Note

Studying language can be glamorous. The words *grammar* and *glamour* have the same etymology. Grammar, a system that describes the structures of a particular language, is derived from the Greek word *gramma* (something written). In medieval Europe, few people could read, and those who could were thought to possess special magical power. The original meaning of *glamour*, which is a variant pronunciation of grammar, was magic or enchantment.

EXERCISES

1. Approximately how many languages are there estimated to be spoken in the world?

_____

2. List at least two ways by which language families are distinguished. _____

_____   _____

3. Name four language families other than Indo-European. _____
_____   _____   _____

4. To which branch of the Indo-European family does English belong?
_____

5. To which branch of the Indo-European family does Latin belong?
_____

6. To which branch of the Indo-European family does Greek belong?
_____

7. What percentage of English vocabulary is derived from Latin and Greek? _____
What percentage of technical vocabulary? _____

8. To which language family does Anglo-Saxon belong? _____
To which branch? _____   Where and when was
it spoken?   _____

9. Name one work written in Old English. _____

10. Anglo-Saxon is a synonym for which language? _____

11. What event introduced a Latin-based vocabulary into English? _____
_____   When did it occur? _____
Through which language did most of these words first pass? _____

12. Who wrote *Canterbury Tales*? _____   To which period of
English does it belong? _____

13. Who is generally credited with the introduction of the printing press into England?
_____   When? _____

14. Who wrote *A Dictionary of the English Language*? _____
When? _____

15. Grammarians have tended to look at what language when establishing rules of English
usage? _____

16. What was the first permanent English-speaking settlement in America? _____
_____

17. During the period 1880–1920, from which area did most of the immigrants to America
come? _____   During the period since 1945?
_____

18. What was Noah Webster's contribution to American English? _____
    _____

19. What is etymology? _____

20. What is linguistics? _____

Temple of Fortune, Rome.

Latin is a dead language,
as you can plainly see.
It killed off all the Romans,
and now it's killing me.

3

HOW LATIN WORKS

Before we can begin to consider the Greek and Latin roots of English vocabulary, we must first understand something of the way in which these languages "work," and how they differ from English.

In modern English, the function of any word in a sentence or a phrase is determined by its position.

EXAMPLE

THE DOG BITES THE MAN.
has a very different meaning from
THE MAN BITES THE DOG.
whereas
THE THE MAN DOG BITES and
BITES MAN THE DOG THE
have no meaning at all.

□

Both Latin and Greek, however, are inflected languages.* That means that the function of words within a particular sentence is determined not by word order, as in English, but by various endings that are placed on each word.

---

*All Indo-European languages were originally highly inflected, although English has lost most of these distinctive endings. We can see the persistence of inflection in English, however, in such changes in form as I, my, me; he, his, him; teach, taught. What does each of these changes indicate?

EXAMPLE

In Latin,
  canis = dog
  vir = man
  mordeo = I bite
If we want to say:
  THE DOG BITES THE MAN.
we may write
  can*is* vir*um* mord*et*, or
  can*is* mord*et* vir*um*, or
  mord*et* vir*um* can*is*, or
  vir*um* can*is* mord*et*.

□

No matter how we arrange the words, the meaning is always the same, because the ending (inflection) of each word determines its function in the sentence. If we want to change the meaning of the sentence, we have to change the endings of the words.

EXAMPLE

If we want to say
  THE MAN BITES THE DOG.
we may write
  can*em* vi*r* mord*et*, or
  can*em* mord*et* vi*r*, or
  mord*et* vi*r* can*em*, etc.

□

What has changed in these different Latin sentences? Can you figure out why these changes have occurred?

LATIN NOUNS AND ADJECTIVES

The changes in the endings of nouns and adjectives are determined by *declension*. Each change of form that occurs is called a *case*. There are six cases in Latin, each one expressing a possible function of a noun, pronoun, or adjective in a sentence.

EXAMPLE

  femina = woman

Case	Form (singular)	Function	Example	Form (plural)
nominative	femina	subject	The woman carries the book.	feminae
genitive	feminae	possessive	I carry the book of the woman.	feminarum
dative	feminae	indirect object	I give the book to the woman.	feminis
accusative	feminam	direct object	I see the woman.	feminas
ablative	feminā	manner/means	I came with the woman.	feminis
vocative	femina	address	Woman, come here!	feminae

There are five declensions (that is, five different sets of endings) in Latin; every noun and adjective belongs to one of these five declensions. Each declension is identified by the ending found in the genitive (possessive) case.

1. The first declension is identified by *-ae* in the genitive case:

   EXAMPLE
   femina, femin*ae* = woman, of the woman*
   porta, port*ae* = door, of the door
   nauta, naut*ae* = sailor, of the sailor

2. The second declension is identified by *-i* in the genitive case:

   EXAMPLE
   vir, vir*i* = man, of the man
   amicus, amic*i* = friend, of the friend
   bellum, bell*i* = war, of the war

3. The third declension is identified by *-is* in the genitive case:

   EXAMPLE
   rex, reg*is* = king, of the king
   mens, ment*is* = mind, of the mind
   urbs, urb*is* = city, of the city

4. The fourth declension is identified by *-ūs* in the genitive case:

   EXAMPLE
   manus, man*ūs* = hand, of the hand

---

*There is no indefinite (a, an) or definite (the) article in Latin.

senatus, senatūs = senate, of the senate
cornu, cornūs = horn, of the horn

☐

5. The fifth declension is identified by -*ei* in the genitive case:

EXAMPLE
fides, fidei = faith, of the faith
dies, diei = day, of the day

☐

There are very few nouns and no adjectives that belong to the fourth and fifth declensions.

FINDING THE STEM OF A LATIN NOUN OR ADJECTIVE

The reason it is so important to understand how declensions work is that almost all English derivatives of Latin nouns and adjectives are formed from the *stem* of the word. The stem of a noun or adjective is the genitive case minus the case ending.

EXAMPLE

genitive case	*stem*
feminae	femin-
nautae	naut-
portae	port-
viri	vir-
belli	bell-
regis	reg-
mentis	ment-
urbis	urb-

☐

LATIN VERBS

Just as nouns and adjectives are inflected, so are verbs. The inflection of verbs is called *conjugation*. The changes in verb endings (inflection) indicate person (1st, 2nd, or 3rd person), tense (time of action), voice (active or passive), and mood (indicative, subjunctive, or imperative).

EXAMPLE

amo = I love   amamus = we love
amas = you love   amatis = you love
amat = he, she, it loves   amant = they love

amor = I am loved
amabit = he (or she or it) will love
amabitur = he (or she or it) will be loved
amavi = I have loved
amatus sum = I (a man) have been loved
amata erat = she had been loved
amemus = let us love
amate = love!

☐

Almost every Latin verb has four stems (called principal parts), each of which has a different function, and from which are formed all the possible tenses, voices, and moods.

EXAMPLE

(1) amo, (2) amare, (3) amavi, (4) amatum
amo = I love (*present*)
amare = to love (*infinitive*)
amavi = I have loved (*perfect active*)
amatum = having been loved (*perfect passive*)

☐

CONJUGATIONS

There are four conjugations, each of which is distinguished by the vowel that appears in the infinitive form:

1. The first conjugation is distinguished by *a* in the infinitive form:

    EXAMPLE
    amo-am*a*re-amavi-amatum = love
    porto-port*a*re-portavi-portatum = carry

☐

2. The second conjugation is distinguished by *ē* (long) in the infinitive form:

EXAMPLE
    moneo-monēre-monui-monitum = warn
    teneo-tenēre-tenui-tentum = hold

3. The third conjugation is distinguished by *e* (short) in the infinitive form:

EXAMPLE
    duco-ducere-duxi-ductum = lead
    ago-agere-egi-actum = do, drive
    facio-facere-feci-factum = make

4. The fourth conjugation is distinguished by *i* in the infinitive form:

EXAMPLE
    audio-audire-audivi-auditum = hear
    venio-venire-veni-ventum = come

FINDING THE STEM OF A LATIN VERB

Almost all English derivatives from Latin verbs are formed either from the present infinitive stem (which is the infinitive minus the *-re* ending) or from the perfect passive stem (the fourth principal part minus the *-um* ending).* Very often, when a suffix is added to the present stem of a verb (see next chapter), the distinguishing vowel of the conjugation is also dropped before the suffix is added.

EXAMPLE

Present infinitive	*Present stem*	*Perfect passive*[†]	*Perfect stem*
portare	porta-	portatum	portat-
monēre	monē-	monitum	monit-

*For this reason, the third principal part of the verb will not be given in subsequent vocabulary.

†The perfect passive form is really an adjective as well as a verb (see p. 33n). Since all nouns and adjectives have *gender* (masculine, feminine, or neuter), every adjective has a masculine, feminine, and neuter form, depending on the gender of the noun it is describing. The form previously given (*-um*) is the neuter form. We shall see in the following chapters the consequences of this dual existence of the participle.

tenēre	tenē-	tentum	tent-
ducere	duce-	ductum	duct-
agere	age-	actum	act-
facere	face-	factum	fact-
audire	audi-	auditum	audit-

Note

There is a class of Latin verbs called *deponent* — verbs that are conjugated with the passive endings only, but that have active meanings. The conjugation to which each deponent verb belongs is identified by the same vowels in the infinitive form already noted. The mark of the passive infinitive is a final *i*.

EXAMPLE

1. The first-conjugation deponent verb is distinguished by an *a* in the infinitive form:
   arbitror-arbitr*a*ri-arbitratum = think
   hortor-hort*a*ri-hortatum = urge

2. The second-conjugation deponent verb is distinguished by an *ē* (long) in the infinitive form:
   fateor-fat*ē*ri-fassum = speak
   mereor-mer*ē*ri-meritum = deserve

3. The third-conjugation deponent verb loses the *er* in the infinitive and has only the *i* as the indication of the infinitive:
   sequor-sequ*i*-secutum = follow
   revertor-revert*i*-reversum = return

4. The fourth-conjugation deponent verb is distinguished by an *i* in the infinitive form:
   experior-exper*i*ri-expertum = try

□

EXAMPLE

Present infinitive	*Present stem*	*Perfect participle*	*Perfect stem*
arbitrari	arbitra-	arbitratum	arbitrat-
hortari	horta-	hortatum	hortat-
fatēri	fatē-	fassum	fass-
merēri	merē-	meritum	merit-

sequi	seque-*	secutum	secut-
reverti	reverte-*	reversum	revers-
experiri	experi-	expertum	expert-

□

USEFUL LATIN VERBS

Principal parts	English meaning	Present stem	Perfect stem
ago-agere-actum	do, drive	age-	act-
amo-amare-amatum	love	ama-	amat-
audio-audire-auditum	hear	audi-	audit-
capio-capere-captum	take	cape- (-cipe-)†	capt- (-cept-)†
cedo-cedere-cessum	go, yield	cede-	cess-
dico-dicere-dictum	say	dice-	dict-
do-dare-datum	give	da-	dat-
duco-ducere-ductum	lead	duce-	duct-
facio-facere-factum	make	face- (-fice-)†	fact- (-fect-)†
fero-ferre-latum	bear, carry	fer-	lat-
loquor-loqui-locutum	speak	loque-	locut-
mitto-mittere-missum	send	mitte-	miss-
moveo-movēre-motum	move	movē-	mot-
pono-ponere-positum	put, place	pone-	posit-
porto-portare-portatum	carry	porta-	portat-
scribo-scribere-scriptum	write	scribe-	script-
sto-stare-statum	stand	sta-	stat-
teneo-tenēre-tentum	hold	tenē- (-tine-)†	tent-
venio-venire-ventum	come	veni-	vent-
video-vidēre-visum	see	vidē-	vis-
voco-vocare-vocatum	call	voca-	vocat-

---

*The present stem of third-conjugation deponent verbs replaces the distinguishing final e that it lost when forming the infinitive.

†In compounds of facio, capio, and teneo, the a or e of the present stem becomes i. In the perfect stem of compounds of facio and capio, the a becomes an e.

EXAMPLE

recipio-recipere-receptum = take back
conficio-conficere-confectum = make together, accomplish
retineo-retinēre-retentum = hold back, retain

□

Notes

Double Meanings

Sometimes, two English words will have the same Latin root, but totally different meanings.

EXAMPLE

egregious and *gregarious* both derive from **grex, gregis** = flock.
salary and *saline* both derive from **sal, salis** = salt.
money and *admonish* both derive from **moneo, monēre, monitum** = warn.

Check your unabridged English dictionary for current meanings of these words and how these meanings developed.

☐

Doublets

When two different English words derive from the same root and have similar meanings but different English spellings, they are called *doublets*.

Doublets occur when a Latin root comes into English in two different ways: directly from Latin and through an intermediary language, such as French, as well.

EXAMPLE

royal and *regal* both derive from **rex, regis** = king.
poison and *potion* both derive from **potio, potionis** = drink.
dainty and *dignity* both derive from **dignitas, dignitatis** = dignity.
card and *chart* both derive from **charta, chartae** = paper.

☐

EXERCISES
(*pages 16–18*)

A. Find the stem of each of the following Latin nouns or adjectives (1–22) and list an English derivative and its meaning. Use your unabridged English dictionary to find the derivative and its definition.

Samples

Latin word	English meaning	Stem	Derivative	Meaning
liber, liberi	free	liber-	liberal	favoring progress

audax, audacis	bold	audac-	audacity	boldness, daring

Latin word	English meaning	Stem	Derivative	Meaning
1. familia, familiae	family	famili	familiar	Often encountrd
2. liber, libri	book	libr	libral	
3. corpus, corporis	body	corpor	corporation	
4. nox, noctis	night	noct	nocturnal	
5. mors, mortis	death	mort	mortal	
6. ars, artis	skill	art	artficical	
7. bellum, belli	war	bell	bell	
8. canis, canis	dog	can	canine	
9. pes, pedis	foot	ped	peddle	
10. lex, legis	law	leg	leg	
11. vulnus, vulneris	wound	vulner	vuln	
12. acer, acris	sharp	acr	acdr	
13. levis, levis	light	lev	levy	
14. fama, famae	rumor, reputation	fam	fame	great reputation
15. os, oris	mouth	or	orfas	
16. os, ossis	bone	oss		
17. gravis, gravis	heavy	grav	gravity	
18. vita, vitae	life	vit	vital	
19. tempus, temporis	time	tempor	temporal	

20. rus,   countryside r u r _____ _____
    ruris
21. rarus,   rare   r a r   rare   _____
    rari
22. vetus,   old   veter   veterain   _____
    veteris

(*pages 18–22*)

B. In Exercises 23–42 fill in the present or perfect stem, derivative, and current meaning of each of the following Latin verbs.

rego-regere-rectum = rule   dormio-dormire-dormitum = sleep
verto-vertere-versum = turn   voco-vocare-vocatum = call
libero-liberare-liberatum = free   fallo-fallere-falsum = deceive
relinquo-relinquere-relictum = leave miror-mirari-miratum = wonder at
sentio-sentire-sensum = feel   nascor-nasci-natum = be born

Samples

Latin verb	Present stem	Derivative	Current meaning
doceo-docēre-doctum	docē-	docile	easily trained or managed
tango-tangere-tactum	tange	tangible	real, actual

Latin verb	Present stem	Derivative	Current meaning
23. rego	rege		
24. verto	verte		
25. libero	libere		
26. relinquo	relinque		
27. sentio	sentie		
28. dormio	dormic		
29. voco	voce		
30. fallo	falle		
31. miror	mir		
32. nascor	nasc		

Samples

Latin verb	Perfect stem	Derivative	Current meaning
doceo	doct-	doctor	a learned person
tango	tact-	tactile	pertaining to touch

Latin verb	Perfect stem	Derivative	Current meaning
33. rego	regt		
34. verto	vert		
35. libero	libert		
36. relinquo	relinqu		
37. sentio	sentit		
38. dormio	dormit		
39. voco	voct		
40. fallo	falle		
41. miror	mos		
42. nascor			

C. The following Latin words (43–57) are used in English without any change in form or ending. Find the original Latin meaning of each word by looking in an unabridged English dictionary. Which of these words have changed in meaning, even when they have remained the same in form?

Latin word	Latin meaning	Current English meaning
43. miser		
44. bonus		
45. pauper		
46. minister		
47. album		
48. arbiter		
49. crux		
50. via		
51. minor		
52. superior		

53. prior   _____   _____
54. gratis   _____   _____
55. onus   _____   _____
56. rancor   _____   _____
57. squalor _____   _____

D. In Exercises 58–72 fill in the blank with the word that best defines the italicized word or part of a word in the sentence. Make sure that your sentences are grammatically correct.

Sample

An *audit*ion allows an actor to be __heard__.

58. An *ag*ile person is able to __move freely__.
59. A *capt*ive is one who has been __taken hostige__.
60. *Data* is information __accumulation__.
61. At a con*ven*tion, the delegates have __meeting__ together.
62. An in*scrip*tion is __written__ upon a tombstone.
63. *Stat*us is an indication of one's social __standing__.
64. A re*ced*ing hairline __regresses__ back on the head.
65. A *ten*ant __rents__ his property.
66. "Please re*mit* payment" is a polite way of saying "__send__ back the money."
67. A *fact*ory is a place where goods are __made__.
68. Trans*port*ation is a means of __moving__ across.
69. A de*posit* is money __put__ down on an item to be purchased.
70. E*locut*ion lessons teach you how to __speak__ out.
71. A con*duct*or __directs__ the orchestra.
72. An individual who is *dict*atorial likes to __tell__ people what to do.

The arch of Septimus Severus, Roman Emperor (A.D. 193–211).

I trade with both the living and the dead, for the enrichment of our native tongue. We have enough in England to supply our necessity, but if we will have things of magnificence and splendour, we must get them by commerce.

JOHN DRYDEN, DEDICATION OF HIS TRANSLATION OF
VERGIL'S *Aeneid* (1697)

LATIN INTO ENGLISH

Just as we form adjectives and nouns in English from other English nouns and verbs (e.g., woman, womanly; farm, farmer; move, movable), so too, did the Greeks and Romans. Each ending (suffix) that we add to the stem of a noun or adjective tells us something about the quality or nature of the word.

I. ADJECTIVAL ENDINGS USED WITH LATIN NOUN STEMS

Latin ending	Meaning	English derivative form
-alis, -ialis	having the characteristic of, belonging to	-al, -ial
-anus, -ianus	having the characteristic of, belonging to	-an, -ian
-aris, -arius	having the characteristic of, belonging to	-ar, -ary
-ilis	having the characteristic of, belonging to	-il, -ile
-inus	having the characteristic of, belonging to	-ine
-osus	full of, abounding in	-ose, -ous
-lentus	full of, abounding in	-lent

EXAMPLE

Latin noun	English meaning	Latin stem	Latin adjective	English derivative
princeps, principis	chief	princip-	principalis	principal
margo, marginis	edge, boundary	margin-	marginalis	marginal

socius, socii	ally, companion	soci-	socialis	social
vox, vocis	voice	voc-	vocalis	vocal
urbs, urbis	city	urb-	urbanus	urban, urbane
mare, maris	sea	mar-	marinus	marine
familia, familiae	family	famili-	familiaris	familiar
vir, viri	man	vir-	virilis	virile
servus, servi	slave	serv-	servilis	servile
copia, copiae	abundance	copi-	copiosus	copious
virus, viri	poison	vir-	virulentus	virulent

Note

Because Latin nouns and adjectives have gender, the Romans commonly used the masculine, feminine, or neuter form of the adjective as a noun, e.g.:

magnus (masculine) = large, but also the large man

magna (feminine) = large, but also the large woman

magnum (neuter) = large, but also the large thing

How do we determine the gender of a noun in the Romance languages?

II. NOUN-FORMING SUFFIXES WITH LATIN NOUNS AND ADJECTIVES

Sometimes we wish to express the abstract quality of a particular noun or adjective, and we do so by forming a new noun (e.g., man, manly, manliness; state, statehood; handsome, handsomeness; kind, kindly, kindliness).

Latin ending	English meaning	English derivative form
-atus	office, group engaged in	-ate
-itas, -ietas	quality of	-ity, -iety
-itudo	abstract state or quality	-itude
-itia	abstract state or quality	-ice
-monium, -monia	abstract state or quality	-mony
-ia, -ium	abstract state or quality	-y
-arium	place where	-arium
-ista	one who believes in	-ist*
-ismus	an abstract belief in	-ism*

*These Latin endings are actually derived from Greek suffixes (see p. 48) and are most often used to form learned borrowings (see p. 35n) in English.

EXAMPLE

Latin noun or adjective	English meaning	Stem	Derived Latin noun	English derivative
princeps, principis	chief	princip-	principatus	principate
brevis, brevis	short	brev-	brevitas	brevity
socius, socii	ally	soci-	societas	society
varius, varii	different	vari-	varietas	variety
virilis, virilis	manly	viril-	virilitas	virility
magnus, magni	large	magn-	magnitudo	magnitude
gratus, grati	pleasing	grat-	gratitudo	gratitude
pater, patris	father	patr-	patrimonium	patrimony
custos, custodis	guard	custod-	custodia	custody
malus, mali	evil	mal-	malitia	malice
servus, servi	slave	serv-	servitudo, servitia	servitude, service
sol, solis	sun	sol-	solarium	solarium

◻

III. DIMINUTIVE-FORMING SUFFIXES WITH LATIN NOUNS

We may indicate the smallness or familiarity of an object or person by the addition of a suffix (e.g., drop, droplet).

Latin ending	English derivative form
-culus	-cule
-ellus	-el
-illus	-il
-olus	-ole
-uleus; ulus	-ule

EXAMPLE

Latin noun	English meaning	Latin diminutive form	English derivative
corpus	body	corpusculus	corpuscle
moles	mass	moleculus	molecule
saccus	bag	saccellus	satchel
pupus	boy	pupillus	pupil (student)
pupa	girl	pupilla	pupil (part of the eye)

gladius	sword	gladiolus	gladiolus
area	ground	areola	areole
nux	nut, kernel	nuculeus	nucleus

□

IV. NOUNS AND ADJECTIVES FORMED FROM LATIN VERBS

We may also make a noun or an adjective from a verb by the addition of a suffix; the newly-formed noun or adjective retains the quality of action in the verb [e.g., make (verb) > > > maker (noun); say (verb) > > > saying (noun)]. In Latin, nouns and adjectives may be formed from either the present or the perfect passive stem of the verb. Remember that the present stem will often lose its final vowel, especially if it is joined to a suffix that begins with a vowel.

i. Nouns and adjectives formed from the present stem of Latin verbs

Latin noun ending	English meaning	English derivative form
-mentum	state of, quality of	-ment
-bulus; -bulum	means of, place of, result of	-ble
-men	means of, place of, result of	-men
-or	means of, place of, result of	-or
-culus; -culum	means of, place of, result of	-cle

Latin adjectival ending	English meaning	English derivative form
-bilis; -ilis	capable of being	-ble, -ile
-ax, acis	inclined to	-acious
-uus; ulus	inclined to	-uous, -ulous
-idus	inclined to	-id
-ns, -ntis (singular)	indicates present participle*	-nt
-ntes or -ntia (plural)	indicates present participle*	-nce or -ncy

---

*A participle is a verb form used as an adjective; the present active participle is indicated most often in English by adding the suffix *-ing* to the simple form of the verb—e.g., the running man, the smiling woman, the driving rain. Because Latin participles are adjectives, they can be declined and have gender and number. All present participles belong to the third declension.

EXAMPLE

Latin verb	English meaning	Present stem	Latin noun or adjective	English derivative form
sto-stare	stand	sta-	stabulum; stabilis	stable (place), stable (adj.), stabile
doceo-docēre	teach	docē-	documentum; docilis	document; docile
specio-specere	look at	spece-	specimen	specimen
rigeo-rigēre	stiffen	rigē-	rigidus; rigor	rigid; rigor
veho-vehere	drag	vehe-	vehiculum	vehicle
audeo-audēre	dare	audē-	audax, audacis	audacious
credo-credere	believe	crede-	credulus; credibilis	credulous; credible
vaco-vacare	be empty	vaca-	vacuus	vacuous
tolero-tolerare	bear	tolera-	tolerans, tolerantis; tolerantia	tolerant; tolerance
ago-agere	do, drive	age-	agens, agentis; agentia	agent; agency
rego-regere	rule	rege-	regens, regentis; regentia	regent; regency
audio-audire	hear	audi-	audientes	audience

□

ii. Nouns and adjectives formed from the perfect passive stem of Latin verbs*

Latin ending	English meaning	English derivative form
-or	he who	-or
-rix	she who	-rix
-ura	act of, result of	-ure
-orius; -orium	that which is used for	-ory; -orium
-ivus	given to	-ive
-io, -ionis	state of, result of, process of	-ion
-ilis	capable of being	-ile

*The fourth principal part of the verb, from which the perfect passive stem is derived, is also a participle, but is passive in meaning, and refers to something that happened in the past. It is most often expressed in English by the suffixes -ed and -en: e.g., *scrambled* eggs (eggs that have been scrambled), a *broken* leg (a leg that has been broken), or a *married* man (a man who has been married). All perfect passive participles in Latin belong to the first and second declensions.

EXAMPLE

Latin verb	Perfect stem	Latin noun or adjective	English derivative
ago-agere-actum	act-	actor; activus; actio, actionis	actor; active; action
doceo-docēre-doctum	doct-	doctor	doctor
sto-stare-statum	stat-	statura; statio, stationis	stature; station
facio-facere-factum	fact-	factorium; factio, factionis	factory; faction
capio-capere-captum	capt-	captor; captivus; captura	captor; captive; capture
audio-audire-auditum	audit-	auditorium; auditor; auditio, auditionis	auditorium; auditor; audition
mitto-mittere-missum	miss-	missio, missionis; missilis	mission; missile

☐

V. VERBAL SUFFIXES

i. The Romans added the verbs *ago, facio,* and *capio* to adjectives and nouns to form new verbs, adjectives, and nouns. The newly-formed verbs then had the meaning to do, make, or take a certain state.

Latin verb	English meaning	Latin compound verb form	English derivative form
ago	do, drive	-igo	-igate; -igation
facio	make, do	-ficio	-fy; -fic; -ficate
capio	take	-cipio	-cipate; -cipation

EXAMPLE

Latin adjective or noun	English meaning	Compound Latin verb	English derivative
castus	pure	castigo (make pure)	castigate; castigation
pax, pacis	peace	pacifico (make peaceful)*	pacify; pacific; pacification
pars, partis	part	participo (take part)*	participate; participation

☐

*Note that in compounds formed from a noun or adjective together with facio or capio, the final *i* of the verb often disappears.

ii. By adding the suffix -sco to a verb stem, noun, or adjective, Latin indicates the process of beginning or continuing.

Latin root	English meaning	Latin compound form	English derivative
candeo-candēre	shine	candesco = begin to shine	candescent; candescence
seneo-senēre	be old	senesco = grow old	senescent; senescence
quies, quietis	rest	quiesco = become quiet	quiescent; quiescence

VI. VERBAL LEARNED BORROWINGS*

There are many learned borrowings from Latin in English that are derived from Latin verb stems:

Latin verb	English meaning	English derivative form	Meaning
facio-facere-factum	make	-fact	made
voro-vorare-voratum	eat	-vore	eater
fero-ferre-latum	carry, bear	-fer	carrier
caedo-caedere-caesum	kill	-cide	killer, killed

EXAMPLE

Latin noun and English meaning	+ English derivative form	= English noun > > >	English adjective
ars, artis (skill)	-fact	artifact	artificial
caro, carnis (flesh)	-vore	carnivore	carnivorous
conus, coni (cone)	-fer	conifer	coniferous
frater, fratris (brother)	-cide	fratricide	fratricidal

□

*A learned borrowing is a word based on a Greek or Latin root, but given a meaning that did not exist in Latin or ancient Greek — e.g., *telephone*, which is formed from two ancient Greek words (tele = from a distance; and phone = sound). The Greeks of the fifth century B.C. obviously did not have telephones, but because of the high esteem in which classical learning was held, the ancient Greek language was used to find a name for this 19th-century invention.

Note

All of the terms that we use to describe the parts of speech are derived from Latin roots.

Noun = a word referring to a person, place, thing, state, or quality
      nomen, nominis = name
      cf. onyma (ὄνυμα) = name

Verb = a word that expresses action, existence, or occurrence
      verbum, verbi = word

EXERCISES

A. Which English adjectives are derived from the following Latin nouns (1–10)? What is the current meaning of each adjective? Use the endings listed in Section I. If necessary, consult an unabridged English dictionary.

Samples

Latin noun	English meaning	English adjective	Current meaning
vulgus, vulgi > > > vulgaris	crowd	vulgar	crude, unrefined
juvenis, juvenis > > > juvenilis	young	juvenile	young, childish

Latin noun	English meaning	English adjective	Current meaning
1. annus, anni	year	annaul	once a year
2. divus, divi	god	divine	~~supreme~~ god like
3. tempus, temporis	time	temporal	short time
4. mundus, mundi	world	mundan	of the world
5. populus, populi	people	population	# of people living in area
6. corpus, corporis	body	corpuse	dead person
7. miles, militis	soldier	military	of a marines
8. fabula, fabulae	story	Fabuless	fairy tail

9. luna, lunae   moon   _lunar_   _of the moon_

10. turba, turbae   crowd   _turbulance_   _character of a cloud_

B. Which English nouns are derived from the following Latin adjectives (11–15)? What is the current meaning of each noun? Use the endings listed in Section II. If necessary, consult an unabridged English dictionary.

Samples

Latin adjective	English meaning	English noun	Current meaning
avarus, avari > > > avaritia	greedy	avarice	greed
fortis, fortis > > > fortitudo	brave	fortitude	moral strength, bravery

Latin adjective	English meaning	English noun	Current meaning
11. potens, potentis	powerful	_potent_	~~strong~~ power
12. brevis, brevis	short	_brevity_	_shortnes_
13. magnus, magni	large	_magnitude_	_make larger_
14. novus, novi	new	_novice_	_beginner_
15. acer, acris	sharp	_acumoney_	_sharpness_

C. The following words (16–25) have been made up, but they have been given Latin adjectival or noun endings. Identify each as either a noun or an adjective, and give the meaning of the suffix.

	Noun or adjective?	Meaning of suffix
16. spragid		
17. fulmatorium		
18. granatary		
19. crellacious		
20. dractator		
21. stractitial		
22. gremulent		

23. lorbimony   _____   _____

24. traminiety   _____   _____

25. agrenience   _____   _____

D. Which English nouns and adjectives are derived from the present stems of the following Latin verbs (26–35)? What is the current meaning of each noun or adjective? Use the endings in Section IV, Part i; and if necessary, consult an unabridged English dictionary.

Samples

Latin verb	English meaning	English noun or adjective	Current meaning
vivo-vivere-victum vive- > > > vividus	live	vivid	intense, full of life
valeo-valēre* > > > valē- > > > valor	be strong	valor	boldness, courage

Latin verb	English meaning	English noun or adjective	Current meaning
26. curro-currere-cursum	run	*current*	*onward movement*
27. experior-experiri- expertum	try	*experience*	*the act of trying*
28. recipio-recipere- receptum	take back	*recipient*	*a person who take back*
29. miror-mirari-miratum	marvel at	*mirorical*	*event to marvel at*
30. stupeo-stupēre*	be stunned	*stuppor*	*the act of being stunned person*
31. oppono-opponere- oppositum	place against	*opponent*	~~something~~ *to place against*
32. rapio-rapere-raptum	seize	*rapacious*	
33. ardeo-ardēre*	burn	*arden*	*incline to burn*
34. alo-alere-altum	nourish	*Alimentary*	*of or pertinting to nourish*
35. sedeo-sedēre-sessum	sit	*sediment*	~~settle to the bottom~~ *somthing that sits*

*Some Latin verbs do not have a perfect passive form.

E. Which English nouns and adjectives are derived from the perfect stems of the following Latin verbs (36–45)? What is the current meaning of each noun or adjective? Use the endings in Section IV, Part ii, and, if necessary, consult an unabridged English dictionary.

Samples

Latin verb	*English meaning*	*English noun or adjective*	*Current meaning*
tolero-tolerare- toleratum > > > tolerat- > > > toleratio	bear, endure	toleration	endurance
jungo-jungere- junctum > > > junct- > > > junctura	join	juncture	act of joining

	Latin verb	*English meaning*	*English noun or adjective*	*Current meaning*
36.	moveo-movēre- motum	move	~~Motions~~	movement
37.	dormio-dormire- dormitum	sleep	dormitory	place to ~~~~ sleeping
38.	nascor-nasci-natum	to be born	native	sone
39.	lego-legere-lectum	choose; speak; read	lecture	~~class~~ act of speaking
40.	curro-currere-cursum	run	cursive current	onward movement
41.	recipio-recipere- receptum	take back	recapture	
42.	sedeo-sedēre-sessum	sit	session ~~sediment~~	sitting settle to the bottom
43.	rapio-rapere-raptum	seize	rapture	seizing
44.	voco-vocare-vocatum	call	vocal	act of calling
45.	video-vidēre-visum	see	vision	~~act of seeing~~

Papyrus containing a magical spell. The serpent swallowing his tail symbolizes the never-ending circle of creation and destruction.

Graecum est. Non potest legi. (It's Greek to me; it can't be read.)

COMMENT OF A MEDIEVAL SCRIBE, WHO COULD NOT DECIPHER THE GREEK WORDS FOUND IN HIS LATIN MANUSCRIPT

HOW GREEK WORKS

GREEK

Like Latin, Greek is an inflected language with declensions and conjugations. Because most English words derived from Greek roots are learned borrowings, or had passed from Greek into Latin before coming into English at a later date, there are not the same strict rules, as there are for Latin-based words, for the formation of Greek-based English vocabulary.

The Greek Alphabet

Greek letter	Greek name	Pronunciation	Transliteration
α, Α (ἄλφα)	alpha	a (short)	a
β, Β (βῆτα)	beta	b	b
γ, Γ (γάμμα)	gamma	g (hard)	g
δ, Δ (δέλτα)	delta	d	d
ε, Ε (ἔψιλόν)	epsilon	e (short)	e
ζ, Ζ (ζῆτα)	zeta	dz	z
η, Η (ῆτα)	eta	a (long)	e or a
θ, Θ (θῆτα)	theta	th	th
ι, Ι (ἰῶτα)	iota	i (short)	i
κ, Κ (κάππα)	kappa	k	c
λ, Λ (λάμβδα)	lambda	l	l
μ, Μ (μῦ)	mu	m	m

ν, Ν (νῦ)	nu	n	n
ξ, Ξ (ξῖ)	xi	x	x
ο, Ο (ὄμικρόν)	omicron	o (short)	o
π, Π (πῖ)	pi	p	p
ϱ, Ρ (ῥῶ)	rho	r	r
σ, ς; Σ (σῖγμα)	sigma	s	s
τ, Τ (ταῦ)	tau	t	t
υ, Υ (ῦ ψιλόν)	upsilon	u	y
φ, Φ (φῖ)	phi	f	ph
χ, Χ (χῖ)	chi	ch	ch
ψ, Ψ (ψῖ)	psi	ps	ps
ω, Ω (ὦ μέγα)	omega	o (long)	o

(handwritten margin notes: "begining or ending", "middle of word")

RULES FOR THE TRANSLITERATION OF GREEK WORDS INTO ENGLISH

1. Diphthongs (two vowels which blend into a single sound):

Diphthong	Transliteration	Greek example	English transliteration
αι	ae, e	φαινόμενον*	= phenomenon
		Αἰθιοπία	= Ethiopia
αυ	au	αὐτό	= auto (self, same)
ει	ei, i, e	χείρ	= chir (hand)
ευ	eu	εὐλογία	= eulogia (praise)
		ψεῦδος	= pseudos (false)
οι	oe, i, e	ἀμοιβή	= ameba or amoeba (change)
ου	ou, u	Μοῦσα	= Muse

2. upsilon (υ) is usually transliterated as *y*.

   EXAMPLE

   κύκλος = cyclos (circle)

   Αἴσχυλος = Aeschylus†

   τύπος = typos (figure, form)

   □

When it is part of a diphthong, however, it is transliterated as a *u*.

---

*Every Greek word has an accent mark, but it does not affect the transliteration of the word into English.

†Many Greek words were borrowed by the Romans and given Latin endings; thus, the Greek *-os* often becomes the Latin *-us*.

EXAMPLE
τραῦμα = trauma (wound)
ψεῦδος = pseudos (false)

☐

3. If a gamma (γ) appears before another gamma, kappa (κ), chi (χ), or xi (ξ), the gamma is pronounced in Greek, and transliterated in English, as an *n*.
    EXAMPLE
    ἄγγελος = angelos (messenger)
    φάλαγξ = phalanx

☐

4. If a word begins with a vowel, that vowel is marked with what is called a *breathing sign*. There are two breathing signs: smooth and rough. If a word has a smooth breathing sign, the vowel is given its original value; if it has a rough breathing mark, it is pronounced and transliterated with an initial *h* before the vowel.

    smooth breathing sign = ᾿   rough breathing sign = ῾

    EXAMPLE
    ἀντί = anti
    ἰῶτα = iota
    ἁρμονία = harmonia
    ὥρα = hora

☐

If a word begins with a rho (ρ), the rho always receives a rough breathing sign, and is transliterated as *rh*.

EXAMPLE
ῥήτωρ = rhetor (speaker)
ῥόμβος = rhombos (rhombus)

☐

COGNATES

Because both Latin and Greek are members of the Indo-European family and therefore have a common ancestry, many Latin words have Greek *cognates* (words that are derived from the same earlier form). Thus, we find the following verbs in Greek that are related to Latin verbs we have already seen on page 22. These verbs have the same meaning.

Latin verb	Greek verb	English meaning
ago	ago (ἄγω)	do, drive
fero	phero (φέρω)	bear, carry
sto	histemi (ἵστημι)	cause to stand

EXERCISES

Transliterate each of the following Greek words according to the rules given in this chapter. Which of these words came into English unchanged? What is the current meaning of each English word?

Greek word	Transliteration	Unchanged?	Current meaning
1. θεός			
2. δρᾶμα			
3. ἵππος			
4. ξένος			
5. ἀμφί			
6. παραβολή			
7. ὑπό			
8. φύσις			
9. λόγος			
10. μέθοδος			
11. παραγραφή			
12. ῥήτωρ			
13. σύνθεσις			
14. τραῦμα			
15. τράπεζα			
16. φαρμακός			
17. χάρισμα			
18. αἴσθησις			
19. λέων			
20. χαρακτήρ			

21. ἀξίωμα

22. βιβλίον

23. πολυγαμία

24. ἔμφασις

25. Ὅμηρος

26. δέρμα

27. ὠκεανός

28. γένεσις

29. βάρβαρος

30. ψώρα

Delphi

Numbering, preeminent among subtle devices,
I found for them, and the combining of letters,
for remembering all things, the mother of the Muses,
skilled in all crafts.

AESCHYLUS (5TH CENTURY B.C. TRAGIC PLAYWRIGHT),
Prometheus Bound

GREEK INTO ENGLISH

GREEK SUFFIXES

Because many Greek-based words in English are learned borrowings, or they passed through Latin before entering into our vocabulary, the rules for their formation are not as regularized as for Latin-based vocabulary. Thus, only those Greek suffixes most frequently found in English are given.

I. ADJECTIVE-FORMING SUFFIXES

Greek adjectival suffix	English meaning	English derivative form
-icos (-ικος); -acos (-αχος); -ticos (-τιχος) -oides (-οειδης)	pertaining to like, having the shape or form of	-ic; -ac; -tic -oid*

EXAMPLE

Greek noun	English meaning	Greek adjective	Derivative form
polis (πόλις)	city	politicos (πολιτιχός)	politic

*The adjectival suffix -oid is often used in English as a learned borrowing to mean "similar to" or "resembling."

cosmos (κόσμος)	order	cosmicos (κοσμικός)	cosmic
		cosmeticos (κοσμητικός)	cosmetic
mania (μανία)	madness	maniacos (μανιάκος)	maniac
sphera (σφαῖρα)	ball	spheroides (σφαιροειδής)	spheroid

II. NOUN-FORMING SUFFIXES

Greek noun suffix	English meaning	English derivative form
-ia (-ια)	quality of	-ia; -y
-ica; -tica (-ικα; -τικα)	art, science, study of	-ics; -tics
-tes (-της)	one who does	-t
-ter, -tor (-τηρ; -τωρ)	one who does	-ter, -tor
-ma (-μα)	result of	-ma; -me; -m
-sis; -sia (-σις; -σια)	result of	-sis; -sy
-eion; -eon (-ειον; -αιον)	place for	-eum; aeum (Latinized form)
-iskos (-ισκος)	diminutive	-isk
-ismos (-ισμος)	abstract quality; belief in; theory of	-ism*

EXAMPLE

Greek noun or verb	English meaning	Greek compound noun	English meaning	English derivative form
apologeomai (ἀπολογέομαι)	defend	apologia (ἀπολογία)	defense	apology
polis (πόλις)	city	politica (πολιτικά)	city affairs	politics
gymnazo (γυμνάζω)	exercise (verb)	gymnastes (γυμναστής)	one who exercises	gymnast

*The noun-forming suffix -ism is often used in English as a learned borrowing to indicate a belief in or adherence to a particular point of view, political, or religious, or otherwise—e.g., communism, realism, Catholicism.

hypocrinomai (ὑποκρίνομαι)	answer, act	hypocrites (ὑποκριτής)	actor	hypocrite
		hypocrisia (ὑποκρισία)	acting	hypocrisy
Musa (Μοῦσα)	Muse	Mouseion (Μουσεῖον)	place of the Muses	museum
aster (ἀστήρ)	star	asteriskos (ἀστερίσκος)	little star	asterisk
baino (βαίνω)	go	basis (βάσις)	step	basis
tithemi (τίθημι)	put, place	thema (θέμα)	deposit	theme
		thesis (θέσις)	putting	thesis

□

III. LEARNED BORROWINGS

The following suffixes are Greek in origin, but most often appear in English as learned borrowings.

Greek base	English meaning	Greek suffix form	English combining form	English meaning
logos (λόγος)	word	-logia	-logy	art, science, study of
cratos (κράτος)	power	-cratia or crasia	-cracy	rule by
			-crat	ruler
		-craticos	-cratic	pertaining to rule by
arche (ἀρχή)	rule*	-archia	-archy	rule by
archon (ἄρχων)	ruler	-archos	-arch	ruler

*arche (ἀρχή) also means beginning, or first in authority. When used as a prefix in English, it usually means "chief," e.g., archbishop, archenemy, architect, etc.

grapho (γράφω)	I write	-graphia	-graph	tool for writing
			-graphy	writing
gramma (γράμμα)	letter	-gramma	-gram	thing written
scopeo (σκοπέω)	I look at		-scope	tool for viewing
			-scopy	viewing
metron (μέτρον)	measure	-metria	-metry	science of measuring
			-meter	instrument for measuring
nomos (νόμος)	law, rule	-nomia	-nomy	rules of; management of
nomicos (νομικός)	conventional	-nomicos	-nomic	pertaining to the rules
-izein (ιζειν)	verb-forming suffix		-ize*	

Note: Anglo-Saxon Suffixes

Not all English suffixes are Greek or Latin in origin. Old English (Anglo-Saxon) has left its mark on the language as well.

Old English suffix	English meaning	Example
-ard	possessor of	dullard
-er, -ster	agent	doer; gangster
-less	without	toothless
-ful	full of	truthful
-some	full of	quarrelsome; toothsome
-ish	somewhat	foolish
-ness	quality of, state of	happiness, largeness
-dom	state of being; domain of	kingdom; martyrdom
-hood	state, condition; character	motherhood; brotherhood

---

*-ize, which denotes action, is frequently used as a learned borrowing in English in the formation of neologisms, such as sanitize, customize, etc.

The poet Homer, to whom the ancient Greeks gave credit for the creation of the *Iliad* and the *Odyssey*.

EXERCISES

A. Transliterate each of the following Greek words (1–10) and, using your dictionary, find an English derivative and its current meaning. Make sure that the root of the English derivative is correct.

Sample

Greek word and English meaning	Transliteration	English derivative	Current meaning
πόλεμος (war)	polemos	polemic	controversial argument

Greek word and English meaning	Transliteration	English derivative	Current meaning
1. τόπος (place)			
2. σχολή (leisure)			
3. ἀγών (contest)			
4. ἔθνος (nation)			
5. κινέω (move)			
6. πρᾶγμα (business)			
7. αἵρεσις (choice)			
8. αἰτία (cause)			
9. ἐκκλησία (assembly)			
10. κλίνη (bed)			

B. Clearly, anyone or anything can rule. What are each of the following forms of governance in Exercises 11–20?

English word	Form of governance	English word	Form of governance
11. gastrocracy		12. plutocracy	
13. patriarchy		14. oligarchy	
15. ochlocracy		16. hierarchy	
17. gynecocracy		18. dyarchy	
19. matriarchy		20. gerontocracy	

C. In Exercises 21–27 fill in each blank with the correct meaning of the italicized word or part of a word. If you are not sure of the derivation, check your dictionary.

Sample

A micro*scope* is a __tool for viewing__ small objects.

21. Geo*logy* is the _____ the earth; geo*graphy* is _____ _____; geo*metry* is _____ _____.

22. An an*archist* _____ an absence of _____.

23. A thermo*meter* allows us to _____ heat.

24. Your *arch*enemy is your _____ foe.

25. In many science-fiction movies, robots are called andr*oid*s because they __*look*__ __*like*__ of humans. [aner, andros (ἀνήρ) = man]

26. Dynam*ism* is _____ that all phenomena in the world can be explained by the action of forces. [dynamis (δύναμις) = force, power]

27. What is the literal meaning of *basilisk*? (βασιλεύς = king) _____ What sort of creature was it? _____ _____

An athletic contest. (Black-figure vase, 6th century B.C.)

And though thou hadst small Latine and less Greeke,
From thence to honour thee, I would not seeke
for names...

BEN JONSON, "TO THE MEMORY OF MY BELOVED,
THE AUTHOR, MR. WILLIAM SHAKESPEARE" (1623)

7

LATIN AND GREEK PREFIXES

Prefixes formed from Latin and Greek prepositions are most often adverbial, that is, they qualify or modify some action that is described by the word to which the prefix is attached.

LATIN PREPOSITIONS

Latin preposition	English meaning	English combining form	Example
ab, a	from, away from	ab-, a-	abduct, avert
ad	to, toward, for	ac-, ad-, af-, ag-, al-, an-, ap-, ar-, as-, at-*	accept, admit, affirm, aggression, allocate, announce, applaud, arrive, assume, attack
ante	before	ante-	antecedent

*Certain consonants (such as *b*, *m*, and *n*) often take on the sound of the following consonant: e.g.,
   sub + pono (place) = suppono, supponere, suppositum (place under)
   cum + laboro (work) = collaboro, collaborare, collaboratum (work together).
This is called assimilation. Sometimes there is only a partial assimilation of sounds: e.g., *n* before *p* becomes *m*:
   in + porto = importo

cum*	with, together	com-, col-, con-, cor-, co-†	compose, collect, convene, correct, cohere
circum	around	circum-	circumnavigate
contra	against	contra-	contradict
de	down, away from	de-	depose
ex, e	out of	ex-, e-	except, edict
extra	outside, outside of	extra-	extraordinary
in	in, into, on	in-, il-, im-	incur, illusion, import
inter	between	inter-	interact
intra	within	intra-‡	intravenous
ob	to; against	ob-, oc-, of-, op-	object, occur, offer, oppose
per	through, by	per-*, pel-	permit, perfect, pellucid
post	after	post-	postpone
prae	before	pre-	predict
pro	in front of; on behalf of	pro-	propose, provide
sine	without, apart	se-	secure, seclude
sub	under; in addition to	sub-, suc-, suf-, sug-, sup-, sus-	submit, success, suffer, suggest, suppose, suspend
super	above	super-	supervise
trans	across	trans-, tra-	transmit, tradition
ultra	beyond	ultra-‡	ultrasonic

GREEK PREPOSITIONS

Greek preposition	English meaning	English combining form	Example
amphi (ἀμφί)	around; on both sides; of both kinds	amphi-	amphitheatre amphibious
ana (ἀνά)	up; backward; again	ana-	anagram analogy
anti (ἀντί)	against	anti-	antidote

*Sometimes *cum* or *per* serve merely to intensify the word to which they are affixed: e.g., per + facio (make, do) > > > perficio, perficere, perfectum = do thoroughly, finish

†co- is most often used as a learned borrowing, meaning "together" or "jointly."

‡In compound form, appears only as a learned borrowing.

apo (ἀπό) or aph* (ἀφ᾽)	from, away from	apo-, aph-*	apology aphorism
cata (κατά) or cath* (καθ᾽)	down; away; against; concerning	cata-, cath-*	catalogue catastrophe catholic
dia (διά)	through	dia-	diameter
en (ἐν)	in	en-, em-	endemic empathy
ec (ἐκ) or ex* (ἐξ)	out of	ec-, ex-*	ecstasy exodus
epi (ἐπί) or eph* (ἐφ᾽)	on, at, for, to; in addition to	epi-, eph-*	epidemic epithet ephemeral
hyper (ὑπέρ)	over, beyond; excessively†	hyper-	hyperbole hyperactive
hypo (ὑπό) or hyph* (ὑφ᾽)	under, below; slightly†	hypo-, hyph-*	hypothesis hyphen
meta (μετά) or meth* (μεθ᾽)	with, after, beyond; change	meta-, meth-*	metabolism metaphysics method
para (παρά)	beside, beyond; contrary to; irregular	para-	paradox parallel paranoia
peri (περί)	around, about, near	peri-	perimeter
pro (πρό)	before, in front of	pro-	prophecy
pros (πρός)	to, toward, in addition to	pros-	prosthesis
syn (σύν)	with, along with	syn-, syl-, sym-, sys-‡	synthesis syllable symphony system

PREFIXES DERIVED FROM GREEK AND LATIN ADJECTIVES AND ADVERBS

Most English compound words formed from the following Greek and Latin adjectives and adverbs are learned borrowings.

---

*Before a word beginning with a vowel marked by a rough breathing, the final consonant of the preposition becomes aspirated (*p > > > ph*; *t > > > th*; *k > > > x*).

†Almost all uses of hyper- and hypo- in English compounds are learned borrowings.

‡In compounds, the *n* of *syn* is often assimilated to the consonant that follows it. (See page 55n.)

Words of Measurement

Greek or Latin word	English meaning	English combining form	Example
magnus, magni	large	magni-	magnify
macron (μαϰϱόν)	large, long, excessive	macro-	macrocosm
multus, multi	much, many	multi-	multiply
poly (πολύ)	much, many	poly-	polygamy
megas (μέγας)	huge	mega-	megaphone
megalos (μεγάλος)	huge	megalo-	megalomania
micron (μιϰϱόν)	small	micro-	microscope
omnis, omnis	all	omni-	omnivore
pan (πᾶν)	all	pan-; panto-	pantheon
			pantomime
homos (ὁμός)	same	homo-	homogenize
homeos (ὅμοιος)	similar	homeo-	homeopathic
aequus, aequi	equal	equi-	equilateral
isos (ἴσος)	equal	iso-	isosceles
auto (αὐτό)	self	auto-	autograph
tele (τῆλε)	far, distant	tele-	telegram
acros (ἄϰϱos)	topmost	acro-	acropolis

Words of Praise

Greek or Latin word	English meaning	English combining form	Example
bene	well	bene-	benefactor
eu (εὖ)	well	eu-	eulogy
philia (φιλία)	love of	phil-, philo-	philanthropy
			philosophy
rectus, recti	straight	recti-	rectify
orthos (ὀϱθός)	straight	ortho-	orthodox

Negatives

Greek or Latin word	English meaning	English combining form	Example
a- (ἀ-)*	not	a-	abyss

*When added to a word that begins with a vowel, an *n* is placed between the prefix and the root word—e.g.,

   a + *arche* (rule) = *anarchy*

in-*	not	in- (il-, im-)	innocuous
			illegal
			immoral
non	not	non-	nonresistant
dis-	apart, away, utterly	dis-	dismiss
malus, mali	bad	male-	malevolent
cacos (κακός)	bad	caco-	cacophony
dys- (δυσ-)	bad, difficult	dys-	dyslexia
miseo (μισέω)	hate	miso-	misogynist
heteros (ἕτερος)	other, different	hetero-	heterogeneous
retro	backward; again	retro-, re-	retrograde
			regressive

Odds and Ends

Greek or Latin word	English meaning	English combining form	Example
archeos (ἀρχαῖος)	old	archeo-	archeology
paleos (παλαιός)	old	paleo-	paleolithic
neos (νέος)	new	neo-	neophyte
cryptos (κρυπτός)	hidden	crypto-	cryptogram
quasi	as if, resembling	quasi-	quasi-official

EXERCISES
(*pages 55–56*)

A. What are the literal and current meanings of each of the following English words (1–25)?

Samples

English word	Literal meaning	Current meaning
convene	come together	assemble, come together
describe	write about	give an account of

English word	Literal meaning	Current meaning
1. abduct	*to take*	*to take from*
2. deduct	*lead down*	*lead away from*
3. conductor	*leader*	*to lead*

*There is no way to distinguish between the use of *in-* as a prefix meaning in or on, or as a negative.

4. transmit _____pass on_____ _____to pass on_____
5. transfer _____~~to~~ crossover_____ _____to cross_____
6. translate _____ _____
7. inscribe _____write on_____
8. predict _____ _____educated guess_____
9. diction _____
10. dictionary _____
11. contravene _____come against_____
12. postpone _____hold off_____
13. accession _____~~to~~ yield_____ _____to yield_____
14. edict _____
15. opponent _____
16. constant _____
17. export _____
18. advise _____
19. circumvent _____
20. defect _____
21. antecedent _____
22. support _____
23. production _____
24. interpose _____
25. extraneous _____

B. In Exercises 26–45 fill in the blanks with the literal meaning of each italicized word or part of a word. Make sure that your sentences are grammatically correct.

Sample

A *promo*tion __moves__ you __in front__ ; a *demo*tion __moves__ you __down__ .

26. At a *colloquium*, individuals ___~~speak~~ talk   together___ one another.
27. An *extra*terrestrial being comes from ___a off___ the earth.
28. *Circumstances* are the events that ___~~happen~~ lead   up to___ an event.
29. Your *supervisor* is ___looking   over___ your work.
30. An *introvert* is an individual who has ___turned   within___ himself.

31. In American history, "*ante* bellum" refers to the period _*befor*_ the Civil War.

32. *Intra*mural sports take place _*within*_ the walls of a school.

33. A *substitute* _____ _____ for you.

34. The *albumen* of an egg is _*white*_.

35. A *credo* is a statement of _*a moral*_.

36. An *agenda* is a list of items to be _*done*_.

37. I was given a *bonus* because I did a _*good*_ job.

38. A person who *interferes* in your business _____ himself _____.

39. When the *onus* of responsibility is placed upon you, it becomes your _*problem*_.

40. A *sinecure* is a job _*without*_ real responsibilities or duties.

41. An *obstacle* _*stands*_ _____ you.

42. A *rancorous* argument is filled with _____.

43. A *viaduct* is the _____ by which water is _____ from one place to another.

44. A person who lives in *seclusion* is closed _____ from the world.

45. A *circumlocution* is a polite way of _____ _____ an unpleasant topic.

(pages 56–57)

C. What are the literal and current meanings of each of the following English words (46–60)? Your dictionary will give you the literal meanings of the original Greek words as well as the current meanings.

	Literal meaning	Current meaning
46. anagram	_____	*God — Dog*
47. catalog	_____	*list down*
48. synthesis	_____	*putting together*
49. perimeter	_____	
50. epigram	_____	*write on*
51. antithesis	_____	
52. hypothesis	*under or below*	*educated guess*
53. paragraph	_____	*witen next to something*
54. parameter	*measure of the sides*	*limiting factor*

55. diametric _____   _____

56. epilogue   _sword in addition to_   _____

57. metaphysics   _beyond the thing of nature_   _____

58. amphibian   _living on both side_   _____

59. prosthesis   _place in addition to_   _____

60. hyperbole   _throw beyond_   _____

D. In Exercises 61–72 fill in the blanks with the literal meanings of the italicized word or part of a word. Make sure that your sentences are grammatically correct.

61. An *amphi*theatre has seats all _around_ .

62. An *apo*state is an individual who stands _away f_____ his faith.

63. A *peri*patetic individual likes to walk _around_____ all the time.

64. When you make a *synthesis* of various ideas, you _place_____ them _together_ .

gen = angle

65. An *anti*dote is given to act _act agains_ a poison.

66. A *dia*gonal is drawn ~~across~~ _through_ an angle.

67. An *epi*taph is written _on_ a tombstone.

68. *Meta*morphosis indicates a _change_ of shape or form.

69. A *para*medic works _beside_ the doctor.

70. A *hyper*critical individual is _over_ judgmental.

71. If you are in a state of *ecsta*sy, you may experience the psychological sensation of _standing_ _out_ your body.

72. A disease that is *en*demic is widespread _in or on_ the people.

E. Some Latin words changed their function when they entered into English. In Exercises 73–82 you are given Latin verb forms that have become English nouns. What are the current meanings of these Latin verbs?

Latin verb	English translation	Current meaning
73. credo	I believe	_____
74. affidavit	he has sworn	_____
75. deficit	it is lacking	_____
76. ignoramus	we do not know	_____
77. placebo	I shall please	_____

78.	recipe	take (imperative)	_____
79.	tenet	she holds	_____
80.	caveat	let him beware	_warring_ _____
81.	caret	it is lacking	_____
82.	fiat	let it be done	_____

(*pages 57–59*)

F. What are the literal and current meanings of each of the following words (83–109)?

Samples

English word	Literal meaning	Current meaning
cacography	bad writing	bad handwriting; incorrect spelling
magnify	make large	make greater in size

	English word	Literal meaning	Current meaning
83.	orthography	*straist writting*	_____
84.	cryptogram	*hidden writting*	_____
85.	megalopolis	*huge ~~city~~/ city*	_____
86.	anarchy	*lack of rule*	_____
87.	malediction	*bad saying*	_____
88.	micrologist	*on who study small things*	_____
89.	omnipotent	*all powerful*	_____
90.	magniloquent	*large speak*	_____
91.	telegram	_____	_____
92.	cacophony	_____	_____
93.	autonomic	_____	_____
94.	panhellenic	_____	_____
95.	paleography	_____	_____
96.	eulogy	_____	_____
97.	paleontology	*study of all thing*	_____
98.	neologism	*new*	_____

99. multitude _state of being, many_ ~~a lot of thing~~ _____
100. rectify _make things right_ _____
101. equity _state of being equal_ _____
102. retroactive ~~the~~ _doing again_ _____
103. impotent _being powerful_ _____
104. homophone _same sound_ _____
105. philology _love of words_ _____
106. isobar _equal weight_ _____
107. misanthrope _man hate_ _____
108. dyslexic _difficult to read_ _____
109. polygraph _many written thing_ _____

G. In Exercises 110–127 fill in the blank(s) with the literal meaning of the italicized word or part of a word. Make sure that your sentences are grammatically correct.

110. An *omnivorous* animal ~~all~~ _eat all_ kinds of foods.

111. If you are a *neophyte* at playing tennis, you may make mistakes because you are _new_ to the sport.

112. A creature that is *macro*cephalic has a _large_ skull.

113. A *miso*gamist is an individual who _hates_ the very thought of marriage.

114. The population of New York City may be said to be *hetero*geneous because it is made up of many _different_ nationalities and ethnic groups.

115. A *bene*volent individual wishes you _well_.

116. A *dys*peptic individual is gloomy and irritable perhaps because she has _bad_ digestion.

117. A *poly*gynist has _many_ wives at the same time.

118. The *Pantheon* was an ancient temple dedicated to _all_ the _gods_.

119. To act *magn*animously is to show that you are generous and therefore have a _large_ spirit.

120. To be *a*bysmally ignorant means that your lack of knowledge is _without_ any measure of depth.

abysmally

121. A *retro*spective exhibit looks _backward_ at the whole of an artist's work.

122. A musical composition that is *euphonious* _sound_ _good_ to the ear.

123. A *micrometer* is an _interment to measure small_ distances.

124. An Anglo*phile* _____ all things English.

125. A *megalo*maniac has a _huge_ sense of his own importance.

126. An *autonomous* state is one that is _self ruling_.

127. Property that has *reverted* to its original owner has been _turn_ _back_ to her.

H. What's in a name? Onyma (ὄνυμα) is the Greek word for name. What is the current meaning of each of the following compounds of onyma (128–134)?

128. acronym _____

129. homonym _____

130. antonym _____

131. synonym _____

132. pseudonym _____

133. anonymous _____

134. cryptonym _____

The Greek hero Heracles, renowned for his enormous strength and violent temper. (6th century B.C.)

T en is the very nature of number. All Greeks and all barbarians alike count up to ten, and having reached ten, revert again to the single unit.

AETIUS (1ST CENTURY A.D. GREEK PHILOSOPHER)

LATIN AND GREEK NUMBERS

The similarities among the words for the numbers one through ten were one of the first clues that led early students of comparative and historical linguistics to posit a common ancestry for the Indo-European family of languages.

Vocabulary

numerus, numeri = number
arithmos (ἀριθμός) = number

LATIN NUMBERS

Cardinal numbers	Roman numerals	English combining form	Example
1. unus	I	uni-	uniform
2. duo	II	duo- or du-	duet
3. tres	III	tri-	triangle
4. quattuor	IV	quadri-	quadrilateral
5. quinque	V	quinqu-	quinquennial
6. sex	VI	sexi- or sex-	sextet
7. septem	VII	sept-	September
8. octo	VIII	oct- or octa-	octet
9. novem	IX	novem- or noven-	November

10. decem	X	decem-	December
100. centum	C	centi- or cent-	centigrade
1,000. mille	M	milli- or mill-	millennium

Examples of Roman Numerals

XI = 11	XIX = 19	XX = 20
XXV = 25	XXXVI = 36	LIII = 53
LXIV = 64	XCIV = 94	CLXXIX = 179
CCX = 210	CCCXLVII = 347	CDXVIII = 418
DLXVII = 567	MDCCCLXXXV = 1885	MCMLXXXIV = 1984

Ordinal numbers	English meaning	Example
primus	first	primary
secundus	second	second
tertius	third	tertiary
quartus	fourth	quart
quintus	fifth	quintet
sextus	sixth	sextuple
septimus	seventh	septimal
octavus	eighth	octave
nonus	ninth	nonagenarian
decimus	tenth	decimal

Numerical adverbs	English meaning	English combining form	Example
sesqui	one and a half	sesqui-	sesquicentennial
bis	twice	bi-	biennial
semi	half*	semi-	semiannual
ambo	both	ambi-	ambidextrous

GREEK NUMBERS

Cardinal numbers	English combining form	Example
1. hen (ἕν) monos (μόνος) = only, alone	heno- mono-	henotheist monogram

*Often used to mean "somewhat" or "partially," e.g., semi-detached.

2. dyo (δύο)	dyo- or dy-	dyad
3. tris (τρεῖς)	tri-	trigonometry
4. tessara or tettara (τέσσαρα, τέτταρα)	tetra-	tetrahedron
5. pente (πέντε)	pent- or penta-	pentathlon
6. hex (ἕξ)	hexa-	hexameter
7. hepta (ἑπτά)	hepta-	heptagon
8. octo (ὀκτώ)	octa- or octo-	octopus
9. ennea (ἐννέα)	ennea-	ennead
10. deca (δέκα)	deca-	decalogue
100. hecaton (ἑκατόν)	hecto-*	hectogram
1,000. chilioi (χίλιοι)	chilo-, kilo-*	chiliastic, kilometer

Ordinal numbers	English meaning	English combining form	Example
protos (πρῶτος)	first	proto-	prototype
deuteros (δεύτερος)	second	deutero-	Deuteronomy

The rest of the Greek ordinal numbers are rarely used in English compounds.

Numerical adverbs	English meaning	English combining form	Example
dis (δίς)	twice	di-	dilemma
hemi (ἡμι-)	half	hemi-	hemisphere

Note

Although they certainly understood the quality of "nothingness," neither the Greeks nor the Romans had a symbol that indicated zero, or the absence of quantity. The arithmetic representation of zero (and the word itself) was introduced by the Arabs.

Vocabulary

Latin word	English meaning
nullus, nullius	no, none
nihil	nothing

---

*Used in English only as a learned borrowing.

EXERCISES

A. Arrange the following words (1–30) in the numerical order indicated by their Latin or Greek roots. What is the meaning of each word? Consult an unabridged English dictionary if you are unsure of the meaning or etymology of any word listed.

English word	Ranking	Meaning
1. trimester	_____	_____
2. hecatomb	_____	_____
3. octagon	_____	_____
4. quintuplet	_____	_____
5. primary	_____	_____
6. duality	_____	_____
7. henotheist	_____	_____
8. September	_____	_____
9. millennium	_____	_____
10. percentage	_____	_____
11. hexagon	_____	_____
12. semester	_____	_____
13. deuteronomy	_____	_____
14. noon	_____	_____
15. monarch	_____	_____
16. unicycle	_____	_____
17. hemisphere	_____	_____
18. tetrarchy	_____	_____
19. novena	_____	_____
20. milligram	_____	_____
21. square	_____	_____
22. dyad	_____	_____
23. decimal	_____	_____
24. century	_____	_____
25. chiliastic	_____	_____
26. quadrangle	_____	_____

27. bigamy   _____   _____

28. hemidemisemiquaver   _____   _____

29. sesquipedalian   _____   _____

30. kilometer   _____   _____

B. In Exercises 31–55 fill in the blank with the literal meaning of the italicized word or part of a word. Make sure that your sentences are grammatically correct.

Samples

To unify a people is to __make__ them into __one__ group.

A *deutero*gamist has married for the __second__ time.

31. *Prim*ates are ranked _____ in the order of living beings.

32. A *tri*logy is a literary work composed of _____ parts.

33. A *quatr*ain is a verse of poetry that has _____ lines.

34. A *sex*tet has _____ members.

35. *Novem*ber should be the _____ month.

36. What is the concern of the Biblical book of *Deuteronomy*? _____

_____

37. When will the *tricentennial* celebration of the United States take place? _____

38. A *proto*type is the _____ model.

39. According to early Christian belief, the *millennium* was to come _____

_____ after the crucifixion of Christ.

40. When a chorus sings in *uni*son, it sings with _____ voice.

41. Poetry written in *hexa*meter has _____ beats to a line.

42. The *penta*gon is a _____-angled building.

43. A *mono*theist believes in _____ god.

44. In exactly two *decades*, what year will it be? Write the answer in Roman numerals.

_____

45. If you are a *sex*tuplet, how many siblings of your age do you have? _____

46. If, after taking this course, you suffer from *sesquipedalianism*, what will be the matter?

_____

47. If the judge declares a contract to be *null and void*, what does this ruling mean?

_____

48. What is the difference in meaning between *ambivalent* and *ambiguous*? _____

_____

49. What is the relationship between a *kilometer* and a *millimeter*? _____

_____

50. When the atomic bomb *annihilated* Hiroshima, Japan, in 1945, it reduced it _____

_____ .

51. A *semiannual* event takes place _____ _____ .

52. A *bi*cameral legislature has _____ chambers of law-makers.

53. To *nullify* a law is to _____ it into _____ .

54. What is the literal meaning of *supernumerary*? _____ What is

its current meaning? _____

55. A *duplicitous* person is deceiving and cunning. What is the root of this word and how

do you think it took on its current meaning? _____

_____

_____

C. What are the French, Spanish, and Italian words for the numbers given in Exercises 56–67?

English	French	Spanish	Italian
56. one	_____	_____	_____
57. two	_____	_____	_____
58. three	_____	_____	_____
59. four	_____	_____	_____
60. five	_____	_____	_____
61. six	_____	_____	_____
62. seven	_____	_____	_____
63. eight	_____	_____	_____
64. nine	_____	_____	_____

65. ten   _____   _____   _____
66. hundred   _____   _____   _____
67. thousand   _____   _____   _____

Portrait bust of Marcus Aurelius, Roman Emperor (A.D. 161–180) and author of the *Meditations*, an exposition of Stoic philosophy.

Finally, I came to the conclusion that the condition of all existing states is bad — nothing can cure their constitutions, but a miraculous reform assisted by good luck — and I was driven to assert, in praise of true philosophy, that nothing else can enable one to see what is right for states and for individuals, and that the troubles of mankind will never cease until either true and genuine philosophers attain political power or the rulers of states by some dispensation of providence become genuine philosophers.

PLATO (4TH CENTURY B.C. GREEK PHILOSOPHER),
Seventh Letter

GOVERNMENT AND POLITICS

GREEK POLITICS

Most modern theories and forms of government (or at least the words that we use to describe them) have their origins in the Greek and Roman political systems. Indeed, the Greeks had a name for every kind of polity, and at one time or another, they seem to have experimented with all of them: monarchy, oligarchy, tyranny, democracy—all these words have etymological roots in Greek political thought.

Greek Political Vocabulary

Greek word	*English meaning*
cybernetes (κυβερνήτης)	pilot, governor
cf.* gubernator, gubernatoris	
polis (πόλις)	city
-cracy	see Greek suffixes, p. 49
-archy	see Greek suffixes
demos (δῆμος)	people
cf. populus, populi	people

*cf., which is used frequently in this text, is an abbreviation of the Latin verb *confer* = compare. Another Latin abbreviation that is often employed is e.g., *exempli gratia* = for the sake of an example.

theos (θεός)	god
cf. deus, dei	
oligoi (ὀλίγοι)	few
aristoi (ἄριστοι)	best, nobility
tyrannos (τύραννος)	absolute ruler
despotes (δεσπότης)	master, lord
ostracon (ὄστρακον)	tile

Ostracism, which now means general exclusion from society or from a particular group, was originally a form of temporary political banishment in Ancient Greece. It was so named because it was voted upon by using as ballots pieces of tile marked "yes" or "no."

ROMAN POLITICS

According to tradition, after the founding of the city by Romulus in 753 B.C., the first form of Roman government was monarchy; but after a revolution and the expulsion of the kings in 509 B.C., a republic was established which lasted until the end of the first century B.C. At that time, in the midst of deteriorating political and social conditions, an imperial form of government began to take root, although republican institutions, such as the Senate and the consulship, survived for many centuries. Of course, the emperor always kept his eye on political matters.

Roman republican and imperial institutions have given their names to many parts of the American system of government. For example, the United States Senate takes its name from the Roman *Senatus*, which originally meant a group of old men, whereas the word "congress" derives from a Latin verb that means "to walk together."

Roman Political Vocabulary

Latin word	English meaning
senex, senis	old man
congredior-congredi-congressus	meet with one another
cf. gradior-gradi-gressum = walk	
volvo-volvere-volutum	turn
rex, regis	king
cf. rego-regere-rectum = rule	
res publica	public matter

publicus is actually a contraction of
  populicus (cf. populus)

civis, civis	citizen
civitas, civitatis	state
imperium, imperii	power, command; empire

  cf. impero-imperare-imperatum
    = command, order; imperator,
    imperatoris = commander,
    emperor

nomino-nominare-nominatum   name
  cf. nomen, nominis = name

Roman Political Offices

consul, consulis = consul, the highest magistrate in the republic
  cf. consulo-consulere-consultum = consider, deliberate

censor, censoris = censor, the magistrate in charge of prosecuting crimes involving
  moral and political offenses, as well as being responsible for the assessment of
  taxes and the raising of revenues for public works
  cf. censeo-censēre-censum = tax, assess

tribunus, tribuni = tribune, the magistrate charged with defending the rights and
  interests of the plebeian class

dictator, dictatoris = dictator. In times of extreme public danger, a dictator might
  be appointed with supreme power by the Senate for a maximum period of six
  months.
  cf. dico-dicere-dictum = say

pontifex maximus = the high priest, who was the head of all the official clergy
  and presided over the religious affairs of the state
  pontifex, pontificis = priest
  maximus, maximi = greatest

ROMAN ECONOMICS

The names of the three social classes of Roman society also have become part of
our political vocabulary. Originally, these divisions were determined by birth; but
in later times, membership in a particular class was often based on wealth.

Vocabulary

Latin word	English meaning
patricius, patricii	patrician, a member of the Roman nobility
cf. pater, patris = father	
eques, equitis	horseman, knight
cf. equus, equi = horse	
plebs, plebis	the common people

The history of the Roman Republic was marked by the struggle of the plebs for political and economic rights.

servus, servi	slave
cf. servio-servire-servitum	
= be a slave	

THEORIES OF SOCIAL AND ECONOMIC ORGANIZATION WITH CLASSICAL ROOTS

All of the following terms that describe modern social and economic systems were coined or developed their present meanings in the 19th and 20th centuries.

Vocabulary

capitalism = caput, capitis (head)

communism = communis, communis (common)

socialism = socius, socii (ally, companion)

fascism = *fasces*, a bundle of sticks with an axe projecting from it, which was carried in front of the chief Roman magistrates, as a symbol both of their power and of the unity of the Roman people

What is the meaning of the suffix *-ism* in each of the preceding terms?

proletariat = proles, prolis (children, descendants)

Those who labor for wages, making their contribution to the state not through the ownership of property, but by the production of children for the labor force.

THE LAW

One of the greatest and most lasting contributions of ancient Roman civilization to the development of Western European thought is the vast body of laws and institutions that form the basis of much of modern jurisprudence. This influence can be seen not only in the structure of many European law codes, but also in the very language of the modern legal system.

Vocabulary

Latin word	English meaning
lex, legis	law
jus, juris	right, law, justice
judex, judicis	judge
cohors, cohortis	enclosure; group, company
crimen, criminis	accusation; the crime of which one is accused
codex, codicis	book

Latin Legal Terminology Used in Modern Law

Latin phrase	English meaning
amicus curiae	friend of the court
bona fide	in good faith
caveat emptor	let the buyer beware
corpus delicti	the body of the crime
cui bono	for which good?
cuius bono	for whose good?
de jure	by law
de facto	by fact
flagrante delicto	while the crime is blazing
habeas corpus	have the body
in camera	in chamber
in loco parentis	in the place of the parent
mandamus	we order
nolle prosequi	be unwilling to prosecute
nolo contendere	I do not wish to contest
obiter dictum	a saying by the way
prima facie	at first appearance
pro bono publico	for the public good
pro forma	according to form
sine die	without a day
alibi	elsewhere, in another place
alias	at another time

Notes

War and Peace

The Roman legal system spread wherever the Roman armies conquered because victory meant the imposition of Roman customs and practices, including, of course, the rule of Roman law. In addition, many veterans, after completing their tours of duty, would settle in the regions where they had been stationed, thus further strengthening Roman control and cultural influence.

Vocabulary

Greek or Latin word	English meaning
bellum, belli	war
polemos [πόλεμος]	war
pax, pacis	peace
miles, militis	soldier
vetus, veteris	old
auxilium, auxilii	help, aid; troops
periculum, periculi	danger
cf. experior-experiri-expertum = try, attempt; risk	
legio, legionis	body of soldiers
cf. lego-legere-lectum = choose	
strategos [στρατηγός]	general
phalanx [φάλαγξ]	body of soldiers

Who's in Charge Here?

Some officers took their titles from the number of men they commanded. How many were overseen by a *decanus*? How many by a *centurio*?

Roman Remains

You can often tell whether an English city was originally a Roman army camp by its name. The endings -caster (as in Lancaster), and -chester (as in Rochester) both come from the Latin *castra*.

Vocabulary

castra, castrorum = army camp

Purity in Politics

The English word "candidate" derives from the fact that when a Roman ran for political office, he would wear a distinctive white toga (*toga candidata*) while campaigning in the Forum.

   cf. candeo-candēre = glow, shine; be clear

Only If the Signs Are Right

Perhaps our political system would operate even more efficiently if we followed the Roman method of making public decisions only when what they regarded as divine signs were favorable. The interpreter of these signs, which included the flight of birds, was called the *augur*, and it was he who decided whether the *auspicia* allowed the Senate to act, a military leader to make an expedition, or a successful candidate to be installed in office or inaugurated.

Vocabulary

augur, auguris = diviner, prophet
auspex, auspicis = one who interprets events through the flight of birds
inauguro-inaugurare-inauguratum = take omens

What's In a Name?

Very often words can take on meanings that are termed pejorative because they imply some sense of disparagement or scorn. The vocabulary of politics is filled with such words. During the 1980s, for example, the word *liberal* was used in some circles in a pejorative sense. But American politicians were not the first to use language in this way. The late Latin word *villanus*, which originally meant a farm laborer, has become our English word "villain." What social attitudes does such a usage reveal?

Vocabulary

pejor, pejoris = worse
villa, villae = country house

Roman forum

EXERCISES

A. In Exercises 1–45 answer each question or fill in the blank. If the sentence needs a word to complete its meaning, make sure that you supply the correct grammatical form.

1. What is a meritocracy? _____

2. What is a plebiscite and who takes part in it? _____

3. What is the science of demography? _____

   _____

4. What was the original purpose of a census? _____

   _____

5. To whom should *regalia* properly belong?_____

6. What happens when *tyrannicide* is committed? _____

7. When I followed the arrow pointing "this way to the egress," where did I end up? _____

   _____

8. Cicero, the Roman statesman, wrote a work entitled *de Senectute*. What was it about?

   _____

9. If a person *pontifi*cates, he speaks in the manner of a _____.

10. A *patri*mony is an inheritance from one's _____.

11. The *imperative* form of a verb indicates a _____.

12. *Civility* is the kind of behavior expected of a _____.

13. The main attractions at an *equestrian* show are the _____.

14. A person who behaves in a *servile* manner acts like a _____.

15. *Per capita* income is measured _____ _____.

16. An *infidel* is a person who is _____ _____.

17. The function of a *legislature* is the _____ of the _____.

18. A *society* is a group that is composed of _____.

19. When a matter is *adjudicated*, it is decided by turning it over _____

    _____.

20. An *aristocrat* believes in the _____ _____.

21. A *progressive* person is willing to _____ _____.

22. A *retrograde* motion is one that _____ _____.

23. Many newspapers claim that they are the *vox populi*. What does that phrase mean?

    _____

24. If you have an *alibi* when a crime has been committed, you are able to prove that you

    were _____.

25. A *demagogue* is a person who is able to _____ _____ by arousing their emotions.

26. What is the difference in meaning between *incriminate* and *recriminate*? _____
_____

27. He crashed into a parked car on the day of his driving test. It was not a very good sign of what was to come; in fact, you might call it _____.

28. What official is chosen in a *gubernatorial* election? _____

29. What is the literal meaning of *metropolis* and what is its current meaning? _____
_____

30. What is the Latin doublet of *royal*? _____

31. What is the literal meaning of *plebeian*? _____ What is its pejorative meaning? _____

32. The *nomin*al head of a committee is chairman in _____ only.

33. If our next president were wise, she would _____ before she was *inaugurated*.

34. If a person speaks with *candor*, he makes his feelings _____.

35. What is the literal meaning of *prolific*? _____ What is its current meaning? _____

36. A *perilous* undertaking is one that places you at _____.

37. The enemy's *bellicose* statements proved that they were ready for _____.

38. *Auxiliary* police are ready to _____ the regular force.

39. A *phalanx* of angry citizens broke into City Hall, looking like a _____.

40. What is the current meaning of *polemic*? _____

41. *Strategy* should be planned by a _____. What is the current meaning of this word? _____

42. *Inveterate* customs are strong because they are _____.

43. They seemed like _____ because of their *militant* actions.

44. If you want to *experi*ence life, you must _____ many things.

45. When the explorer Balboa saw the *Pacific* Ocean for the first time, he gave it this name because he mistakenly thought it was _____.

B. What is the literal meaning of each of the following words (46–59); what is its current meaning?

English word	Literal meaning	Current meaning
46. populous		
47. politic		
48. politics		
49. economics		
50. consulate		
51. imperial		
52. senility		
53. remand		
54. regicide		
55. digression		
56. oligarchy		
57. demotic		
58. censure		
59. jurisdiction		

Relief of Cupid, god of Love, and Psyche, the mortal girl whom he loved.

Why should a man fear where events of chance rule,
and there is clear foreknowledge of nothing?
It is best to live without plan, however one might.
Do not fear marriage with your mother;
for many men already have laid with their mothers in dreams.
But these things are nothing to the man who bears life easily.

SOPHOCLES (5TH CENTURY B.C. TRAGIC PLAYWRIGHT),
Oedipus Tyrannos

PSYCHOLOGY

MODERN PSYCHOLOGY

The modern study of psychology includes the investigation of human (and animal) behavior in all its forms and manifestations, although most laymen tend to view it in the context of the psychoanalytic theories of human action and motivation developed by Sigmund Freud, Carl Jung, and their successors. The language of psychology has so permeated our contemporary vocabulary that many of these terms have lost their original, narrowly conceived, and specialized meanings. Like the terminology of all the modern sciences and technologies, the vocabulary of psychology is based primarily on learned borrowings from Greek and Latin.

Vocabulary

Greek or Latin word	*English meaning*
psyche (ψυχή)	spirit, soul
In compound form, this is used as a prefix.	
psycho- = mind	
In the earliest usage of the word *psychology*	
in English (17th century), it meant the	
study of things concerning the soul.	
animus, animi	soul, mind, courage, passion
anima, animae	breath

mens, mentis	mind*
non compos mentis = not of sound mind	
sanus, sani	healthy, sound
persona, personae	mask
id	it
ego	I
libido, libidinis	desire (cf. liber, liberi = free)

ANCIENT PSYCHOLOGICAL THEORY

In the classical world, many writers found their source material in ancient myths that vividly described the often complex psychological relationships established, developed, and maintained within the structure of the family. The Oedipal complex, as presented by Freud and based on the fifth-century B.C. play *Oedipus Tyrannos* by Sophocles, is perhaps the most famous expression of such conflict; but Greek myth provides us with many other examples of the consequences of familial passions, examples which still seem to be psychologically valid 2500 years later.

Thus, the study of classical myth has provided an illumination of the wellsprings of human action for modern students of psychology, many of whom see as a primary aim of Greek myths the exposition and resolution of the desires, needs, and conflicts that continue to drive us. Several characters from Greek myth, because of their extreme behavior, have given their names to a variety of psychological syndromes. Here are just a few:

narcissism: excessive admiration of one's own physical or mental qualifications. The handsome Narcissus was punished by the gods for his pride and self-absorption. Caused by Nemesis, the goddess of retribution, to fall in love with his own reflection in a pool, he could not bear to tear himself away, and thus faded into nothingness. All that remained was the flower that carries his name.

Electra complex: In psychoanalytic theory, those symptoms said to be caused by suppressed sexual love of a daughter for her father. Electra, daughter of King Agamemnon, conspired with her brother, Orestes, to murder their mother, Clytemnestra, after Clytemnestra slew the king.

---

*mens, mentis survives in the Romance languages as an adverbial ending—e.g., *dolcemente* (Italian) and *dulcemente* (Spanish) and *doucement* (French), all of which mean "sweetly," are derived from the Latin phrase *dulci mente* (with a sweet mind).

Oedipus complex: according to Freud, the desire of the child for sexual gratification with the parent of the opposite sex. The child often exhibits an intense dislike of the other parent. Oedipus, as you will recall, unwittingly (perhaps) killed his father and married his mother.

Vocabulary

Family member	*Latin word*	*Greek word*
mother	mater, matris	mater (μάτηρ)
father	pater, patris	pater (πατήρ)
sister	soror, sororis	adelphe (ἀδελφή)
brother	frater, fratris	adelphos (ἀδελφός)
son*	filius, filii	
daughter	filia, filiae	
family	familia, familiae	genos (γένος) or genea (γενεά)
	gens, gentis	

Love and Marriage

In Greek myth, marriage often proves to be dangerous, indeed, even fatal: Clytemnestra killed her husband Agamemnon upon his return from the Trojan War, although some argued it was with good cause. He had sacrificed their daughter Iphigeneia before setting off for Troy, and then brought back a Trojan princess, Cassandra, as part of his booty. Medea had obtained the Golden Fleece for the Greek hero Jason after he promised to marry her; but she murdered their children when Jason threatened to divorce her in order to marry another woman.

Vocabulary

Greek or Latin word	*English meaning*
matrimonium, matrimonii	marriage
gamos [γάμος]	marriage
nuptiae, nuptiarum	wedding
maritus, mariti	husband
uxor, uxoris	wife
matrona, matronae	married woman
gamete [γαμετή]	wife
gametes [γαμέτης]	husband

*There are no English derivatives from the Greek words for son and daughter.

divortium, divortii   divorce
    cf. verto-vertere-versum = turn
repudium, repudii   divorce
    cf. pudeo-pudēre-puditum = feel shame

WORDS OF EMOTION

Love and Desire

Greek or Latin word	English meaning
amo-amare-amatum	love
amor, amoris	love
phileo (φιλέω)	love
bonus	good
felix, felicis	happy
clemens, clementis	mild, kindly
salax, salacis	lustful
prurio-prurire-pruritum	itch, burn
amicus, amici	friend
eros (ἔρως)	love
verus, veri	true
fidelis, fidelis	faithful
lenis, lenis	soft, smooth
pulcher, pulchri	beautiful
lascivus, lascivi	playful
cupido, cupidinis	desire

Hatred

Greek or Latin word	English meaning
odium, odii	hatred
despicio-despicere-despectum	despise
cf. specio = look at	
abhorreo-abhorrēre	shudder at
cf. horreo = bristle	
miseo (μισέω)	hate
as learned borrowing, used	
as prefix, *miso-*	
inimicus, inimici	unfriendly
cf. amicus	

hostis, hostis	enemy
malus, mali	evil
cacos (κακός)	bad
turpis, turpis	wicked
fallo-fallere-falsum	deceive
mendax, mendacis	lying
pseudos (ψεῦδος)	lie
as learned borrowing, used	
as prefix, pseudo-	
deformis, deformis	ugly
cf. forma, formae	
= shape, form, beauty	

Love Means You Never Have to Say You're Sorry

Vocabulary

Greek or Latin word	English meaning
culpa, culpae	fault, blame
pecco, peccare, peccatum	make a mistake
erro, errare, erratum	stray, wander
delinquo, delinquere, delictum	fail, commit a crime
hybris [ὕβρις]	shamelessness; exaggerated pride
infamia, infamiae	shame, disgrace
cf. fama, famae = rumor, reputation	

Of course, our emotions and behavior may seem to others to be abnormal, and one person's fear may be another's madness or uncontrollable desire.

Vocabulary

Greek or Latin word	English meaning
mania (μανία)	madness
phobos (φόβος)	fear
terreo-terrēre-territum	frighten

THE FOUR HUMORS

In antiquity and in the Middle Ages it was commonly believed by medical practitioners that the body contained four different fluids, or humors. These four humors, when in proper balance, produced good health; but an excess or deficiency of any one of them could cause both physical and mental illness. Even today, derivatives of these words are not only used to describe moods and personality types, but have become part of the modern medical vocabulary.

Vocabulary

Greek or Latin word	English meaning
chole (χολή)	yellow bile
bilis, bilis	bile
melancholia (μελαγχολία)	black bile
cf. melas (μέλας) = black	
phlegma (φλέγμα)	phlegm
sanguis, sanguinis	blood

STAR WARS

There were other theories of personality and behavior in antiquity. For example, many people believed (and still do) that the planets and other heavenly bodies affected human behavior and health, and that individuals born under the signs of particular planets had the temperaments of the gods who ruled over those planets. The planets were named for the gods who were said to have ruled over them.

The Planets and Their Roman Gods

Mercurius, Mercurii = Mercury (the winged messenger of the gods, who was always on the move)

Venus, Veneris = Venus (the goddess of love and sexual desire)

Mars, Martis = Mars (the god of war)

Juppiter, Jovis = Jupiter, also called Jove (the ruler of the gods, who had every reason to be happy)

Saturnus, Saturni = Saturn (a god of agriculture and also a ruler of the gloomy underworld)

Luna, Lunae = the Moon, whose changes in form and shape were believed to affect people's behavior (the sun and the moon were regarded as planets in antiquity)

But other gods could affect human and animal behavior. Pan, the Greek god of flocks and herds, liked to play his pipes in the countryside; the high, shrill notes would cause the animals to act in peculiar ways. It was also said that he could overcome his enemies merely by shouting, for his cry would cause them to feel sudden, unreasonable terror—hence, panic.

SCIENCE AND THE HUMAN MIND

Of course, society today is obsessed and fascinated by precision and scientific measurement, even in the realm of human behavior. Modern psychology has devised all sorts of means to analyze how and why we act, and has developed systems by which human intelligence is thought to be accurately measured. The Greeks and Romans were not so precise as we try to be, but we still use their vocabulary to describe levels of intellectual abilities. Who knows? Perhaps the Greeks and Romans were smarter than we are.

Vocabulary

intellego-intellegere-intellectum = understand, distinguish
   cf. lego-legere-lectum = choose, read
idiotes (ἰδιώτης) = private citizen
  The word was applied to those who cared only for their private affairs, and who were ignorant of public affairs; thus, its meaning became pejorative.
   cf. idios (ἴδιος) = one's own. Used as a prefix in English, idio- = peculiar to
imbecillis, imbecillis = weak
   cf. baculum, baculi = staff, stick
moros (μωρός) = foolish, stupid

Good, Better, Best

The comparative and superlative forms of Latin adjectives can also have English derivatives.

Positive	Comparative	Superlative
malus, mali = bad	pejor = worse	pessimus = worst
bonus, boni = good	melior = better	optimus = best
superus, superi = above	superior = higher	supremus or summus
cf. preposition super		= highest or last
parvus, parvi = small	minor/minus = smaller	minimus = smallest
magnus, magni = large	major = larger	maximus = largest

multus, multi = much, many	plus, pluris = more	plurimus = most
ulter, ultri = beyond	ulterior = farther	ultimus = farthest, last
cf. preposition ultra		

The preceding adjectives are irregular in the formation of their comparative and superlative forms; the regular superlative ending is *issimus* (-issima, -issimum). How does that ending appear in the various Romance languages?

Be Nice to Your Mother

The Latin expression, *alma mater*, which means "nourishing mother," was the term used by ancient Romans to describe their country. Today we apply the phrase to the schools that we attended because their role is to foster and nourish us. When you graduate you can say that, having been nourished by education, you are an *alumnus* (male; pl. alumni) or alumna (female; pl. alumnae). Both *alma* and *alumnus* are derived from

alo-alere = nourish

EXERCISES

A. In Exercises 1–49 answer each question or fill in the blank(s).

1. What does a *magnify*ing glass do? _____   _____

2. Philosophers have always argued about the *summum bonum*. What is it?

    _____   _____

3. Where should your *superiors* be? _____

4. The *minimum* hourly wage is the _____ amount one can be paid.

5. The *mayor* of the city is supposed to have _____ power than the citizens.

6. In the counting of votes, what is the difference between a *plurality* and a *majority*?

    _____

    _____

7. Someone who is *demented* is _____ his _____ .

8. Our *person*alities are really _____ .

9. If you should murder your brother, you will have committed _____ .

10. In a *soror*ity, the members consider themselves to be _____ .

11. *Inclement* weather is _____ _____.

12. *Felix* the Cat is always _____.

13. If you name your dog *Fido*, you would expect him to be _____.

14. What is a *matriarchy*? _____

15. What is a *misoneist*? _____

16. What is a *misogynist*? _____

17. *Cupid* was the Roman god of _____.

18. *Inanimate* objects do _____ have _____.

19. *Genealogy* is the _____ _____.

20. What is the difference between *sanguine* and *sanguinary*? _____

_____

21. A person with a *martial* disposition enjoys _____.

22. An *egotist* is a person whose favorite pronoun is _____.

23. A *sophomore* is really a _____ _____.

24. If you feel *animosity* toward someone, you are _____.

25. *Filial* affection is felt by _____ or _____.

26. What is the difference in meaning between *amiable* and *amicable*? _____

_____

27. To *ameliorate* a situation is to make it _____.

28. We _____ _____ on *despicable* behavior.

29. When the philosophers search for the eternal *verities*, they are looking for those ideas that are always _____.

30. A person guilty of *mendacity* has _____.

31. What is the meaning of the Latin phrase *persona non grata*? _____

_____

32. An *ultimatum* is a _____ proposal or demand.

33. A *pessimist* is always sure that the _____ will happen.

34. *Idio*syncratic behavior is _____ an individual.

35. The motto of the United States is *e pluribus unum*. What does this phrase mean?

_____

36. The *prenuptial* celebration took place _____ _____.

37. *Aberrant* behavior _____ _____ what is normal.

38. Their wedded bliss was shattered when he committed *uxoricide*. What did he do? _____

_____

39. He was *delinquent* in his account, for he had _____ to pay his bill.

40. He was held to be *culpable* for the accident because it was agreed that the collision had been his _____.

41. What kind of cell is a *gamete*? _____

42. When I *repudiated* my former beliefs, I _____ myself from them.

43. Her *impudent* manner indicated that she felt _____ _____.

44. My exam was *impeccable*; I had not made a single _____.

45. His *hybristic* attitude was a clear indication of his _____.

46. What is the current English meaning of *matrimony*? _____

47. What is the current English meaning of *patrimony*? _____

48. The court ruled that he had committed *bigamy* when it was discovered that he had

_____ _____.

49. His *infamous* behavior brought _____ to his family.

B. In Exercises 50–64 define each of the following fears, madnesses, or desires.

50. monomania   _____   51. egomania   _____

52. megalomania   _____   53. dipsomania   _____

54. pyromania   _____   55. kleptomania   _____

56. gamophobia   _____   57. agoraphobia   _____

58. xenophobia   _____   59. acrophobia   _____

60. claustrophobia _____   61. bibliophilia   _____

62. ailurophobia _____   63. pedophilia   _____

64. hematophobia _____

C. By now, you should be able to recognize Romance-language cognates of Latin words. Without consulting a dictionary, see if you can figure out the English meanings of each of the French, Spanish, or Italian words given in Exercises 65–76.

65. rey (noun)   _____   66. amore (noun)   _____

67. amigo (noun) _____   68. padre (noun)   _____

69. fille (noun) _____

70. popolo (noun) _____

71. odio (noun) _____

72. haber (verb) _____

73. con (preposition) _____

74. personne (noun) _____

75. triste (adjective) _____

76. dios (noun) _____

Aqueduct at Caesarea, built by the Romans in the 2nd century A.D. during their occupation of Palestine.

For if it were proposed to all peoples to choose the best customs out of all, after close examination, they would each choose their own as best.

HERODOTUS, iii.38

THE SOCIAL SCIENCES

In most college and university catalogs, the departments of political science and psychology can be found under the heading of the social sciences, those disciplines whose practitioners observe, analyze, and formulate theories about the behavior of people in specific groups and situations, individuals in their relationship to others, and the aetiology (causation) of other kinds of social phenomena. Some of the social sciences are relatively new—the term *sociology* was first used to mean the scientific study of society in the early 19th century—while others, such as anthropology, have their roots in the ancient Greek curiosity about the non-Greek world.

Vocabulary

Greek or Latin word	English meaning
socius, socii	ally, companion
servo-servare-servatum	watch; protect; keep
aetia (αἰτία)	cause
phenomenon (φαινόμενον)	a thing come to light; appearance. In scientific terminology, the learned borrowing pheno- = shining
lyo (λύω)	untie
cf. solvo-solvere-solutum	loosen, untie, release
theoria (θεωρία)	spectacle; comtemplation
situs, sitūs	position, place

divido-dividere-divisum	separate, allot
> > > individuus	not separable
termino-terminare-terminatum	limit; fix, set

SOCIOLOGY

Sociology uses the methodologies of both empirical investigation and systematic analysis in order to determine the origins and functions of organized communities, and the significance of their social institutions and cultural identities.

Vocabulary

Greek or Latin word	English meaning
hodos (ὁδός)	way, path
empiros (ἔμπειρος)	experienced
vestigium, vestigii	trace, track
systema (σύστημα)	the whole; composition
orior-oriri-ortum	rise, come forth
> > > origo, originis	source
fungor-fungi-functum	perform, do
organon (ὄργανον)	instrument, tool; bodily organ
signum, signi	sign, seal, mark
idem	the same

ECONOMICS

Although the ownership of real property remained the aristocratic standard of wealth until the end of antiquity, as early as the second millennium B.C., Greek merchants grew prosperous by trading with the various peoples who lived around the shores of the Mediterranean, while Greek adventurers who had hired themselves out as mercenaries brought back some of the remarkable wares of Egypt and the East. Some historians have suggested that the Trojan War, far from being a battle over the beautiful Helen, was merely a struggle over competing economic spheres of influence. The high finances of bonds, stock options, and mergers and acquisitions may have been unknown to the Greeks and Romans, but lucrative trade, commerce, and speculative investment flourished in the classical world.

Because the land was poor, and perhaps because life at home was sometimes dangerous, sometimes dull, the Greeks often left home to seek their fortunes. Perhaps the most famous Greek adventurer was the mythical hero Odysseus, but others sought an easier and, perhaps, more profitable life in Asia Minor, the home not only of the legendary king Midas, but of Croesus, the 6th century B.C. Lydian king who is credited with having invented money.

The conquests of Alexander the Great in the fourth century B.C. extended the Greek view as far as India; and where the Greek armies went, traders and merchants soon followed. Although Alexander's empire did not outlast his lifetime, contact between East and West remained strong in the Roman period; and the profits generated by the negotiations and contracts for the sale of agricultural products, such as grain and olive oil, as well as the demand for expensive luxury goods, allowed at least a few Romans to accumulate a great deal of money. The government held the monopolies on some industries, but by and large, business was a matter of "caveat emptor."

Those few Romans who could afford it (and some who could not) often indulged in conspicuous consumption and an opulent lifestyle; consumer debt and fraud were probably invented by the Romans, and by late antiquity, inflation was rampant and prices sky-high. Money-lenders charged usurious rates of interest to those who were insolvent and on the edge of bankruptcy. A coherent public fiscal policy, including a budget, seems to have been nonexistent throughout most of Roman history, although in order to meet its obligations, the state raised money through a variety of means, including, of course, taxation. The eventual collapse of the Roman economy is a depressingly all-too-familiar story.

Vocabulary

Greek or Latin word	English meaning
ecos (οἶκος)	house. As a learned borrowing in scientific terminology, eco- = environment
lucrum, lucri	profit, advantage
copia, copiae	abundance
proprius, proprii	characteristic, possession
> > > proprietas, proprietatis	
spero-sperare-speratum	hope
> > > prosper, prosperi	fortunate, favorable
finio-finire-finitum	limit, fix; close
speculor-speculari-speculatum	watch, observe
cf. specio-specere-spectum	look at
vestis, vestis	clothes, garment, covering
> > > vestio-vestire-vestitum	dress, cover

Greek or Latin word	*English meaning*
opto-optare-optatum	choose; wish for
merces, mercedis	pay, wages
cf. mercor-mercari-mercatum	trade
mereo-merēre-meritum	earn, deserve
emporion (ἐμπόριον)	market
pecunia, pecuniae	money
cf. pecus, pecoris	flock, herd
peculium, peculii	private property
mergo-mergere-mersum	sink, overwhelm; cover
fortuna, fortunae	chance, luck; fate
ager, agri	field. As a learned borrowing, agro- = soil, crop
otium, otii	leisure
> > > nec (not) + otium = negotium	business
traho-trahere-tractum	draw, drag
sumo-sumere-sumptum	take, use
debeo-debēre-debitum	owe
fraus, fraudis	deceit
pendo-pendere-pensum	hang
flo-flare-flatum	blow
pretium, pretii	price
premo-premere-pressum	press
cumulus, cumuli	pile
proficio-proficere-profectum	advance; obtain; acquire
Which Latin verb is the base of this word?	
rumpo-rumpere-ruptum	break
utor-uti-usus	use
> > > usura, usurae	interest
fiscus, fisci	basket; purse; treasury
thesauros (θησαυρός)	treasury
fiducia, fiduciae	trust, confidence; security
cf. fides	faith
haereo-haerēre-haesum	stick, cling to
tribuo-tribuere-tributum	give, pay
taxo-taxare-taxatum	tax
cf. tango-tangere-tactum	touch
ligo-ligare-ligatum	tie, bind
labor-labi-lapsum	fall down, slip

Notes

The social sciences sometimes make a claim for the relevance and applicability of their models to the solution of human social problems. Nevertheless, despite the efforts of sociologists, political theorists, economists, and other social thinkers, we are still faced with the paradox that our scientific study of human behavior, in all its forms, has not yet produced the ideal society. Perhaps, sadly, the 16th century philosopher Sir Thomas More was correct in calling his ideal society *Utopia*.

Vocabulary

Greek or Latin word	English meaning
levo-levare-levatum	lighten, lift
plico-plicare-plicatum	fold
modus, modi	measure, manner, way

Much more elegant synonyms for the Latin-based *model* are the Greek-based *paradigm* and *schema*:

paradigma (παράδειγμα)	pattern
schema (σχῆμα)	form, shape, figure
idea (ἰδέα)	form, class, kind
topos (τόπος)	place
ou (οὐ)	not

And in conclusion, now a word from our sponsor?

The ancient economy seems to have managed quite well without the aid of advertising, subliminal or otherwise, although some of the Roman emperors probably could have used some media enhancement and better public-service announcements to improve their image.

Vocabulary

Latin word	English meaning
claudo-claudere-clausum	close
in compounds, -cludere, -clusum	
spondeo-spondēre-sponsum	pledge

limen, liminis	threshold
medium, medii	middle; in the open; public
nuntio-nuntiare-nuntiatum	announce
imago, imaginis	copy, likeness

EXERCISES

A. In Exercises 1–56 answer each question or fill in the blank(s).

1. *Empirical* knowledge comes from _____.

2. An *asocial* person wishes to live _____ _____.

3. The teacher said I was a *paradigm* of good behavior, a _____ to be followed.

4. A museum con*servator*'s job is to _____ works of art.

5. These few _____ of grandeur were the only *vestiges* of my former wealth.

6. *Analysis* allows one to _____ _____ a subject.

7. An artifact found *in situ* has been left _____ _____ where it originally belonged.

8. A planet's *period* of rotation is the measure of how long its _____ _____ its axis takes.

9. What are the different meanings of *individual* and *individuation*?

    (a) _____

    (b) _____.

10. When I was notified that my employment was *terminated*, I knew that my job had

    _____.

11. An *appendage* _____ _____ a body.

12. If you find yourself in a *desperate* situation, you have thrown _____ _____.

13. A *systemic* infection affects the _____ of the body.

14. A person who is *dysfunctional* _____ _____.

15. When I was *absolved* of the crime, I was _____ _____ any blame.

16. An *infinite* number has _____ _____.

17. A *significant* event _____ _____ on history.

18. When he was *elevated* to the title of general, he was _____ _____ the ranks.

19. When asked to *mod*erate her voice, she began to speak in _____ tones.

20. The country's *mercantile* interests were concerned only with _____.

21. As the boat *submerged*, it _____ _____ the water.

22. She gave me a *schematic* drawing of the machine, so that I could see its _____.

23. The Romans called the East the *Orient* because it was in this direction that the sun

    _____.

24. A *presumption* is _____ _____ any facts are known.

25. An *agronomist* studies the _____ _____.

26. In order to get the job, he needed the re*quisite* skills that were being _____.

27. An *impecunious* individual has _____ _____.

28. *Tangible* results are able to be _____.

29. A person with an *abrupt* manner tends to _____ _____

    others.

30. If you have *repressed* an idea, you have _____ it _____.

31. What are *vested* interests? _____ What

    is the root, and how did *vested* acquire this meaning? _____

    _____

32. A *mercenary* individual is interested only in _____.

33. What is the literal meaning of *topography*? _____

    What is its current meaning? _____

34. An *otiose* individual has too much _____.

35. A *medi*ating principle helps us to find the _____ ground.

36. *Fortuitous* events happen by _____.

37. Our *tactile* sense is stimulated by _____.

38. An *adherent* _____ _____ his beliefs.

39. New York City is an *emporium* because it is a center for many different _____

    _____.

40. *Liga*ments are tissues that _____ the organs of the body in place.

41. In a *conflated* story, many accounts have _____ _____.

42. An individual with a *heterodox* position holds a _____ _____

    from the majority.

43. I have become *proficient* in tennis because I have _____ during practice.

44. An *intractable* problem is _____ _____ _____

    to conclusion.

45. A person guilty of *peculation* has taken another person's _____.

46. To *appropriate* an idea is to take it _____ _____.

47. I _____ a con*tribution* to my favorite charity.

48. A *prosperous* person is _____ _____ _____ the future.

49. A *lucrative* business is one that shows a _____.

50. When his illness *relapsed*, his condition _____ _____.

51. I got a *merit* increase in my paycheck, because my work _____ it.

52. You could tell by his *opulent* lifestyle that he was _____.

53. We now use the word *mediocre* in a pejorative way. What is its current meaning? _____ What is its literal meaning? _____

54. We hold life to be *precious* because of its inherent _____.

55. You *defrauded* me of my money when you took it _____ by _____.

56. There was a *copious* supply of food because last year the crops had been _____ _____.

B. Everywhere I turn...

What is the literal meaning of each of the following words (57–61); what is its current meaning?

English word	Literal meaning	Current meaning
57. subversion	_____	_____
58. convert	_____	_____
59. perverse	_____	_____
60. obvert	_____	_____
61. diversionary	_____	_____

C. "Fold in" the following prefixes...

What is the literal meaning of each of the following words (62–68); what is its current meaning?

English word	Literal meaning	Current meaning
62. replication		
63. supplicate		
64. implicate		
65. complicated		
66. quadruplicate		
67. applicant		
68. compliant		

D. It all depends on how you look at it...

What is the literal meaning of each of the following words (69–73); what is its current meaning?

English word	Literal meaning	Current meaning
69. introspective		
70. perspicacity		
71. prospective		
72. spectacular		
73. retrospect		

Asclepius, Greek god of healing, effecting a cure.

Life is short, the art (of medicine) long, the moment fleeting, the attempt dangerous, and judgment difficult.

HIPPOCRATIC CORPUS

HUMAN BIOLOGY AND MEDICINE, I

Perhaps no other area that affects our lives demonstrates so clearly the influence of Greek and Latin on English vocabulary as does the field of medicine. Although new diseases are being defined and new technologies established every day, medicine has created for itself an inexhaustible source for an expanding terminology by consistently drawing upon Greek and Latin roots.

THE HUMAN BODY

The human biological and medical sciences have thoroughly investigated the workings and dimensions of the human body. They have taught us that the body is a wonderful machine that is extraordinarily efficient (most of the time); it is composed of over 200 bones, 700 muscles, approximately five quarts of blood, and covered by about 25 square feet of skin. In addition, it possesses a remarkably intricate nervous system, as well as a multitude of organs that carry on vital, sustaining functions within the machine.

Vocabulary

English word	Latin word	Greek word	Greek compound form*
body	corpus, corporis	soma, somatos (σῶμα)	somato-

*Almost all English compound forms derived from Greek that are used in medical terminology are learned borrowings.

109

bone	os, ossis	osteon (ὀστέον)	osteo-
muscle	musculus, musculi	mys, myos (μῦs)	myo-
blood	sanguis, sanguinis	hema, hematos (αἷμα)	prefix = hema- or hemato-; suffix = -emia
skin	cutis, cutis	derma, dermatos (δέρμα)	dermato-
nerve	nervus	neuron (νεῦρον)	neuro-
life	vita, vitae cf. vivo-vivere = live	bios (βίos)	bio-

Like all machines, however, the human body is subject to occasional breakdowns (despite the classical ideal of *sana mens in corpore sano*). When this happens, we go to see a doctor; and, sometimes, we may even end up as patients in a hospital.

Vocabulary

Greek or Latin word	*English meaning*
hygieia (ὑγίεια)	health
salus, salutis	health
sanus, sani	healthy
doceo-docēre-doctum	show, teach
medicus, medici	healer
iatros (ἰατρός)	doctor, physician
patior-pati-passum	suffer, endure
cf. pascho (πάσχω) = suffer, endure, from which is derived pathos (πάθos) = suffering, misfortune	
-logist	learned borrowing, meaning specialist cf. -logy
hospes, hospitis	host, guest, stranger

MEDICAL SPECIALISTS

Today, of course, most doctors are specialists. There are seemingly as many different specialties in medicine as there are parts of the human body, but we can get to the heart of the matter if we are willing to be patient. Let's start at the top and come face to face with what may be bothering us.

Vocabulary

English word	Latin word	Greek word	Greek compound form
head	caput, capitis	cephale (κεφαλή)	cephalo-
brain	cerebrum, cerebri	encephalos (ἐγκέφαλος)	encephalo-
eye	oculus, oculi	ophthalmos (ὀφθαλμός)	ophthalmo-
ear	auris, auris	ous, otos (οὖς)	oto-
nose	nasus, nasi	rhis, rhinos (ῥίς)	rhino-
mouth	os, oris	stoma, stomatos (στόμα)	stomato-
tooth	dens, dentis	odous, odontos (ὀδούς)	odonto-
tongue	lingua, linguae	glossa (γλῶσσα)	glosso-

There are doctors who attempt to straighten us out or get us back on our feet:

Vocabulary

Greek word	English meaning
skeletos (σκελετός)	dried up; mummy
orthos (ὀρθός)	straight
therapeia (θεραπεία)	service
pous, podos (πούς)	foot
cf. Latin pes, pedis = foot	

There are doctors who specialize in the diseases of particular organs:

Vocabulary

English word	Latin word	Greek word	Greek compound form
heart	cors, cordis	cardia (καρδία)	cardio-
lung	pulmo, pulmonis	pneumon (πνεύμων)	pneumo-
belly	stomachus, stomachi	gaster, gastros (γαστήρ)	gastro-
	abdomen, abdominis	enteron (ἔντερον)	entero-
liver		hepar, hepatos (ἧπαρ)	hepato-
kidney	renum, reni	nephros (νεφρός)	nephro-

or in particular age groups or in a particular gender:

Vocabulary

English word	Latin word	Greek word
child	puer, pueri (boy)	pes, pedos (παῖς)
woman	femina	gyne, gynecos (γυνή)
man	vir, viri	aner, andros (ἀνήρ)
man; mankind	homo, hominis	anthropos (ἄνθρωπος)
old man	senex, senis	geron, gerontos (γέρων)

AN OUNCE OF PREVENTION

Although modern medicine emphasizes the prevention of disease through immunization, vaccination, diet, and good health habits, many things can go wrong. The medical profession, however, offers a variety of approaches that can be used to diagnose, treat, and cure illness, or at least to alleviate it.

Vocabulary

Greek or Latin word	English meaning
munus, muneris	gift, reward
vacca, vaccae	cow
cf. vaccinus = belonging to cows	
dieta (δίαιτα)	way of life

Diagnosis and Treatment

Vocabulary

Greek or Latin word	English meaning
gnosis (γνῶσις)	knowledge
cf. nosco-noscere-notum = know	
cura, curae	care, cure
remedium, remedii	cure, relief
cf. *medicus*	
contagio, contagionis	touching, contact
cf. tango-tangere-tactum = touch	
opsis (ὄψις)	sight
cf. opteuo (ὀπτεύω) = see, look at	
scopeo (σκοπέω)	examine

-osis*	diseased condition of, state of
-itis*	inflammation of
-oma*	swelling
-iasis*	diseased condition of
-pathy Learned borrowing from Greek; cf. pathos (πάθος). In compound form, used as a suffix = disease, condition. Also used in names of systems or methods of treating diseases, e.g., osteopathy.	diseased condition; form of treatment
-plegia Learned borrowing from Greek plege (πληγή) = blow. In compound form, used as a suffix.	paralysis
-algia Learned borrowing from Greek algos (ἄλγος). In compound form, used as a suffix.	pain
-odynia Learned borrowing from Greek odyne (ὀδύνη). In compound form, used as a suffix.	pain
-rrhea Learned borrowing from Greek rheo (ῥέω = flow). In compound form, used as a suffix.	flow or discharge
-gen Learned borrowing from Greek genos (γένος = birth; source). In compound form, used as a suffix to mean production of.	production of
-genic In compound form, used as a suffix to mean producing.	producing
trauma, traumatos (τραῦμα, τραύματος)	wound
frango-frangere-fractum	break
virus, viri	poison
bacterion (βακτήριον) cf. bacillus, bacilli = small staff	rod, staff
fungus, fungi cf. sphongos (σφόγγος) = sponge	sponge
chir (χείρ) In compound form, used as a prefix = chiro-.	hand
manus, manūs	hand
esthesis (αἴσθησις)	perception, feeling
-tomy	cutting, incision

---

*These endings were used in ancient Greek to form nouns; they have been arbitrarily assigned these particular meanings in modern medical terminology.

Learned borrowing from Greek tomos ($\tau o\mu\acute{o}s$) = cutting. In
  compound form, used as a suffix.
  cf. -ectomy = cutting out, removal

-stomy   making an opening
  Learned borrowing from Greek. In compound forms, used as a
  suffix.
  cf. stoma = opening

TO SLEEP, PERCHANCE TO DREAM

Sometimes, all it takes is a good night's sleep to make us feel better —

Vocabulary

Greek or Latin word	*English meaning*
valeo-valēre	be strong
cf. valesco. What does the suffix -sco indicate?	
hypnos ($\H{v}\pi\nu os$)	sleep
coma ($\kappa\hat{\omega}\mu\alpha$)	deep sleep
somnus, somni	sleep; personified by the Romans as a god of sleep
sopor, soporis	deep sleep
Morpheus	the son of Somnus, the bringer of dreams, and given this name because of the various forms he could assume. cf. morphe ($\mu o\varrho\phi\acute{\eta}$) = form, shape

but, not always.

Vocabulary

Greek or Latin word	*English meaning*
mors, mortis	death
cf. morior-mori-mortuum = die	
thanatos ($\theta\acute{\alpha}\nu\alpha\tau os$)	death

Remember: *De mortuis, nil nisi bonum*. (About the dead, nothing but good.)

THE HIPPOCRATIC OATH

The oath that medical students take today has its origins in Greek medicine. Called the Hippocratic Oath, it is named for one of the most famous of ancient Greek healers, Hippocrates.

> I swear by Apollo, the healer, by Asclepius, by Hygieia and Panacea and all the divinities of healing, and call to witness all the gods and goddesses that I may keep this oath and promise to the best of my ability and judgment...that I will use my power to help the sick to the best of my ability and judgment; I will abstain from harming or wronging anyone by it.
>
> ...If, therefore, I observe this oath and do not violate it, may I prosper both in my life and my art, gaining good repute among all men for all time. If I transgress and forswear this oath, may my lot be otherwise.

Vocabulary

Apollo = the Greek god of light, prophecy, healing

Asclepius = the half-divine son of Apollo, patron of Greek physicians. Not content with healing the sick, he attempted to bring the dead back to life. For this act, Zeus struck him down with a thunderbolt.

Hygieia = the Greek goddess of health

Panacea = "All-Healer," said by some to be the daughter of Asclepius

Notes

Scribble, scribble!

By the way, those illegible letters that doctors so often scrawl on prescription forms are abbreviations of Latin phrases:

Abbreviation	Latin phrase	Meaning
ad lib.	ad libitum	as desired
b.i.d.	bis in die	twice a day
h.s.	hora somni	at bedtime
p.o.	per os	by mouth
q.i.d.	quater in die	four times a day
s.o.s.	si opus sit	if necessary
stat.	statim	immediately

Shake, Rattle, and Roll

Many bones of the human body derive their names from their seeming resemblance to other objects. For example, the collar bone, or clavicle, was thought by early anatomists to resemble a key, while the Latin flute was called a tibia because of its similarity in form to the shinbone.

Vocabulary

Latin word	English meaning
clavus, clavi	key > > > collarbone
tibia, tibiae	shinbone > . > > flute
patella, patellae	small pan > > > kneecap
fibula, fibulae	clamp > > > leg bone that extends from knee to ankle

Dig in your heels!

Sometimes a word goes through so many changes of meaning that its original root is unnoticed. *Recalcitrant*, which now means unmanageable or stubborn, is derived from the Latin calx, calcis = heel of the foot. The verb *recalcitrare* originally meant to kick back one's heels, and was applied to horses.

Or change your mind!

Some words are nice to know just because they sound so interesting. *Tergiversate* means to change one's mind or opinion, but its literal meaning is derived from

    tergum, tergi = back
    verso-versare-versatum = turn

If you don't turn your back on an idea, you may turn your mind toward it in a critical way. Thus, we have the verb *animadvert*, which originally meant merely to take notice of, but which has now come to mean to criticize, or to pay attention in a negative manner.

Looks can wound and words can hurt!

A supercilious person is contemptuous of others and demonstrates it by raising his eyebrows.

    supercilium = eyebrow

Sarcastic words can literally tear at our skin.

sarx, sarcos (σάρξ, σαρχός) = flesh > > >
sarcazo (σαρχάζω) = tear flesh

Ave atque vale!

The Roman equivalent of "have a good day" was the phrase "ave atque vale." Although both imperative verb forms mean "be well" or "be strong," they also came to be used as a word of greeting or of good-bye. Thus, the phrase is often translated as "Hail and farewell!"

aveo-avēre = be well
valeo-valēre = be strong, be brave

EXERCISES

A. In Exercises 1–55 answer each question or fill in the blank(s).

1. A *sanguivorous* individual _____ _____.

2. What is the Latin cognate of sympathy? _____.

3. A *corpuscle* is a _____ _____.

4. What is kept in an *ossuary*? _____

5. *Psychosomatic* medicine investigates the interaction of the _____

   and _____.

6. What are the literal and current meanings of the following words?

English word	*Literal meaning*	*Current meaning*
empathy		
sympathy		
apathy		
antipathy		

7. A *subcutaneous* injection is given _____ _____.

8. A *corpulent* person is _____ _____.

9. A *vivacious* person is _____ _____

10. A *patient* is supposed _____ his illness.

11. If you move to a *salu*brious climate, it is hoped that your _____ will improve.

12. What are the following medical specialties?

dermatology _____

hematology _____

neurology _____

13. A *sanitarium* is _____ people hope to become

_____ .

14. The Latin cognate of *hypodermic* is _____ .

15. If a person's beliefs have become *ossified*, they have been _____ as hard as _____ .

16. *Anthropology* is the _____ _____ .

17. It is possible that the Roman poet P. Ovidius *Naso* had a large _____ .

18. *Binoculars* enable us to use _____ _____ .

19. Someone who is *cerebral* uses her _____ .

20. What is the distinguishing feature of a *centipede*? _____ an *octopus*? _____ a *tripod*? _____ a *biped*? _____

21. What skill does a *multilingual* person have? _____ _____ a *polyglot*? _____ _____

22. *Rhinoplasty* is an elegant name for a _____ _____ .

23. An electro*encephalogram* _____ the activity of the

_____ .

24. A *pulmonary* function test measures the capacities of your _____ .

25. A *captain* is the _____ of a military unit.

26. *Cordial* feelings arise from the _____ .

27. A *ophthalmoscope* is _____ .

28. A *periodontist* takes care of the area _____ _____ .

29. A *gastronome* is _____ his _____ .

30. An object that is *auri*form is shaped like an _____ .

31. What are the following medical specialties:

    gerontology _____

    podiatry _____

    otorhinolaryngology _____

    ophthalmology _____

    nephrology _____

    psychiatry _____

    gastroenterology _____

32. A person suffering from *megalocardia* has _____ _____ .

33. What is the literal meaning of *anemia*? _____

34. If your spouse said, "Let's osculate," what should you be prepared to do? _____
    _____

35. An *androgynous* creature displays the characteristics of both _____
    and _____ .

36. A *mortuary* is _____ _____ .

37. *Odontalgia* is an elegant name for _____ _____ .

38. A *traumatic* experience is one that _____ you.

39. The 19th-century poet William Cullen Bryant wrote a work entitled "Thanatopsis."
    What was its theme? _____

40. A *prognosticator* thinks that he can _____ the future _____
    it happens.

41. *Iatrogenic* illness is _____ _____ .

42. A *chiropodist* uses his _____ to take care of your
    _____ .

43. A *manuscript* is a document that has been _____ by
    _____ .

44. A *sinecure* is a job _____ _____ .

45. An *agnostic* says that the proof of the existence of an ultimate cause is _____
    _____ .

46. If your teacher's lecture acts as a *soporific* it may _____ you
    _____ .

47. *Aesthetics* is the _____ _____.

48. A *post mortem* examination is done _____ _____.

49. If you undergo an *encephalectomy*, your _____ has been

_____ .

50. A *curator* _____ _____ objects in a museum.

51. A *valedictory* address is one that _____ _____.

52. "To be in the arms of *Morpheus*" is an elegant way of saying that you are _____ .

53. An *equivalent* dosage of medicine is one of _____

_____ .

54. What is the literal meaning of *pedagogy*? _____

What is its current meaning? _____

55. A *somniloquist* _____ while still _____ .

B. People and things can be broken in a number of ways. What are the meanings of the words given in Exercises 56–60?

56. fragment _____   57. fraction _____

58. fractious _____   59. refract _____

60. infraction _____

C. Analyze the diseases and conditions given in Exercises 61–70.

61. pericarditis _____

62. hematoma _____

63. enteritis _____

64. hepatitis _____

65. dermatomyositis _____

66. polymyalgia _____

67. rhinorrhea _____

68. hemiplegia _____

69. neuropathy _____

70. encephalitis _____

Roman sarcophagus for a child. Found at the Turkish city of Adana.

The ordinary man should adopt the following regimen. During the winter, he should eat as much as possible, drink as little as possible, and this drink should be wine as undiluted as possible.

HIPPOCRATIC CORPUS

13

HUMAN BIOLOGY AND MEDICINE, II

In the preceding chapter, we surveyed all the major organs of the human body as well as the variety of ailments that might afflict them; but for those who wish to continue their medical education, what follows is an overview of the major systems, or structures, to which those organs belong. Once again, Greek and Latin roots provide the necessary language for labeling their various components and operations. Although many of these terms have come into English unchanged, some of the words that are included in this chapter are learned borrowings. Indeed, ancient Greek and Roman physicians sometimes had an imperfect understanding not only of human anatomy, but of the functions of various organs and systemic processes.

Note: Medical and anatomical terms already given in Chapter 12 are not repeated here.

THE CIRCULATORY SYSTEM

The circulatory, or cardiovascular, system consists of the heart and blood vessels.

Vocabulary

Greek or Latin word	English word	Original meaning (if different)	Compound form
vena, venae	vein		veno-
phleps, phlebos (φλέψ)	vein		phlebo-

arteria (ἀϱτηϱία)	artery	windpipe (because it was believed that the arteries carried air)	arterio-
vas, vasis	vessel		vasculo-
corona, coronae	coronary	crown	corono-
lympha, lymphae	lymph	fluid; water	lympho-, lymphato-

THE RESPIRATORY SYSTEM

The function of the respiratory system is to take in and utilize oxygen and to give off carbon dioxide.

Vocabulary

Greek or Latin word	English word	Original meaning (if different)	Compound form or English adjective
spiro-spirare-spiratum	breathe		
pneo (πνέω)	breathe		pneo-
jugulum, juguli	throat		jugular
pharynx (φάϱυγξ)	throat		pharyngo-
trachea (τϱαχεῖα)	windpipe	rough (the adjective used to describe the "artery" that carried air)	tracheo-
bronchia (βϱόγχια)	bronchia (passageway for air to and from lungs)	windpipe; duct	bronchio-
pleura (πλευϱά)	pleura (membrane enfolding lungs)	side; rib	pleuro-
diaphragma (διάφϱαγμα) or phren* (φϱήν)	diaphragm	partition or midriff	phreno-

THE DIGESTIVE SYSTEM

The digestive system encompasses all the organs necessary for taking in, breaking down, and absorbing food.

---

*The *phren* was thought to be the seat of the emotions and the source of mind. As a result, the compound form *phreno-* is used to denote words related either to the diaphragm or the mind.

Vocabulary

Greek or Latin word	English word	Original meaning (if different)	Compound form or English adjective
digero-digerere-digestum	digest	separate, divide	digestive
pepto (πέπτω)	digest	soften; cook; digest	peptic
intestinum, intestini	intestine	internal; intestine	intestinal

The intestine, or alimentary canal, is divided into two parts, the small and large intestine. The small intestine consists of:

Vocabulary

Greek or Latin word	English word	Original meaning (if different)	Compound form or English adjective
pyloros (πυλωρός)	pylorus	gate-keeper	pyloro-
duodeni	duodenum*	twelve	duodenal
jejunum, jejuni	jejunum	hungry, dry; barren	jejuno-
ileum, ilei	ileum	flank	ileo-

The large intestine consists of:

Vocabulary

Greek or Latin word	English word	Original meaning (if different)	Compound form or English adjective
caecum, caeci	cecum	blind; concealed	cecal
colon (χόλον)	colon		colo-
rectum, recti	rectum	straight	recto-

There are several other major organs whose secretions aid in the digestion of food:

Vocabulary

Greek or Latin word	English word	Original meaning (if different)	Compound form or English adjective
cholae (χολαί)	gall bladder		cholecysto- (see under)

---

*The duodenum gets its name from its size, about 12 finger-breadths in length.

pancreas (πάγκρεας) pancreas sweetbread (literally, pancreato all flesh)

There are, of course, many words in both Greek and Latin that have to do with eating, some of which have become part of modern medical vocabulary:

Vocabulary

Greek or Latin word	English word	Compound form or English adjective
phagein (see under *The Digestive System*)	eat	-phage; phago-
edo-edere-esum	eat	
trophe (τροφή)	food	-trophy
nutrio-nutrire	nourish	
orexis (ὄρεξις)	appetite	-orexia
geusis (γεῦσις)	taste (noun)	-geusia

USEFUL BEGINNINGS AND ENDINGS

The following Greek-based prefixes and suffixes are used in modern science and medicine to describe other systems, functions, and components of the body:

Vocabulary

English compound form	Greek root	Current meaning	Original meaning
adeno-	aden (ἀδήν)	denoting a gland	gland
-blast; blasto-	blastos (βλαστός)	denoting a germ or seed	sprout; seed
-cyte; cyto-	cytos (κύτος)	denoting a cell	hollow
cyst; cysto-	cystis (κύστις)	denoting a sac	bladder
histo-	histos (ἱστός)	denoting tissue	web
myelo-	myelos (μυελός)	denoting bone marrow	marrow
tricho-	thrix, trichos (θρίξ, τριχός)	denoting hair	hair

All the following prefixes are derived, with no change in meaning, from Greek adjectives; they are used in biology and medicine to describe a variety of physical characteristics:

Vocabulary

Greek adjective	Meaning	English compound form
brachys (βραχύς)	short	brachy-
bradys (βραδύς)	slow	brady-
leptos (λεπτός)	slender	lepto-
malacos (μαλακός)	soft	malaco-
pachys (παχύς)	thick	pachy-
platys (πλατύς)	broad	platy-
scleros (σκληρός)	hard	sclero-
tachys (ταχύς)	fast	tachy-
xeros (ξηρός)	dry	xero-

EXERCISES

A. In Exercises 1–20 what are the following diseases, medical procedures, or biological processes?

1. venotomy _____

2. arteriogram _____

3. vasculitis _____

4. phlebectomy _____

5. tracheostomy _____

6. pleurodynia _____

7. dysgeusia _____

8. tachycardia _____

9. cholecystitis _____

10. brachypnea _____

11. anorexia _____

12. trichotillomania _____

13. osteomalacia _____

14. adenoma _____

15. myelopathy _____

16. histogenesis _____

17. colonoscopy _____

18. pharyngoplegia _____

19. pancreatalgia _____

20. schizophrenia _____

B. In Exercises 21–37 fill in the blank with the literal meaning of the underlined word or part of word:

21. He was so aggressive that when he "went for the *jugular*," everyone around him covered their _____ .

22. A *platypus* is a mammal distinguished by its _____ _____.

23. A *pachyderm* is an animal distinguished by its _____ _____.

24. A *dyspeptic* individual is grouchy perhaps because he has _____

_____.

25. A *sclerotic* individual is one whose ideas have become _____.

26. The queen received a _____ at her *corona*tion.

27. His *inspiring* speech allowed me to _____ _____ his knowledge and wisdom.

28. What is the meaning of *atrophy* in medical terminology? _____

What is its meaning in the following sentence? "Her desire for fame and fortune faded as her acting career *atrophied*." _____

29. A *pneometer* is an _____ _____.

30. A *leptorrhine* individual has a _____ _____.

31. A *brachycephalic* individual has a _____ _____.

32. A snail may be called a *bradykinetic* creature because it moves _____

_____.

33. The trademark *Xerox* was given to a process of making _____ copies.

34. An omo*phagous* animal _____ raw food.

35. The *pylorus* acts as a _____ between the stomach and duodenum.

36. *Cytology* is the _____ _____.

37. The *lymphatic* system is composed mainly of _____.

C. The Latin verb *digero* is a compound of *gero-gerere-gestum* = bear, carry. What are the literal and current meanings of the following words (38–43)?

	Literal meaning	Current meaning
38. egest	_____	_____
39. ingest	_____	_____
40. congestion	_____	_____
41. gestation	_____	_____
42. gesture	_____	_____
43. suggestive	_____	_____

D. Some parts of the body derive their names from ancient misconceptions about human anatomy. Check your dictionary to find out how the following body organs got their names (44–45):

44. jejunum _____

45. artery _____

Roman Colosseum

*T*he gods did not reveal all things to men from the beginning, but in time by seeking, men find out better.

XENOPHANES (6TH CENTURY B.C. PHILOSOPHER)

SCIENCE AND MATHEMATICS

Most of the vocabulary of modern science and technology is derived from Greek and Latin roots. Many of these terms are, of course, learned borrowings, since the ancient world's concepts of, and postulates about, physical reality were quite different from those of modern science. Nevertheless, the questions that the ancient Greeks and Romans asked about the nature of the world—how it worked and of what sort of material it was made—determined the course of scientific inquiry until the modern period; the recognition that the Greeks and Romans were the founders of the Western intellectual tradition led the modern physical sciences to reach back to their classical roots in order to construct their specialized vocabularies.

Vocabulary

Greek or Latin word	*English meaning*
scio-scire-scitum	know
episteme (ἐπιστήμη)	knowledge, science
techne (τέχνη)	skill
ars, artis	skill, art
physis (φύσις)	nature
natura, naturae	nature
cf. nascor-nasci-natum = be born	
hyle (ὕλη)	matter
materia, materiae	matter

quaero-quaerere-quaesitum	ask
in compounds, -quirere, quisitum	
postulo-postulare-postulatum	demand, ask
quantum, quanti	how much?
qualis, qualis	of what kind?
quot	how many?

ASTRONOMY

One branch of science, astronomy, does have very strong links to antiquity, since the heavens were studied with great interest and enthusiasm by the ancients; and many of the terms used by modern astronomers were employed first by the Greeks and Romans, although often within a different context. For example, when a modern astronomer uses the word "planet," she means any heavenly body that shines by reflected light and revolves around a sun; but the ancient definition of a planet was any of the heavenly spheres that had apparent motion. These, then, included the sun and the moon, as well as Mercury, Venus, Mars, Jupiter, and Saturn—but not the Earth.

Some of the terminology of astronomy has its origins in Greek mythology. We call the system of stars to which our sun belongs the Milky Way because traditionally, the Greeks told the story that it had been formed from drops of milk [gala, galactos (γάλα) = milk] spilled from the breast of the goddess Hera as she was nursing the infant hero Heracles. Hence, too, of course, the word *galaxy*. In addition, many of the constellations are named for figures who appear in Greek and Roman myth.

In the ancient world, scientific astronomy and astrology coexisted quite happily. Many believed (then as now) in astrology, which maintained that the meaning of the present and the future could be revealed through the study of the activity of the planets and the stars. According to traditional astrological theory, the interrelationship between the planets and the constellations, or the signs of the Zodiac, exerts a special influence over human affairs. And even if we do not believe in the validity of astrology, it has given us words that we normally do not associate with the stars: *disaster*, *dismal*, and *influenza*.

Although many ancient Greek philosophers and scientists rejected the basic premises of astrology, they did believe that the universe was perfect and unchanging, the visible symbol of a divine order; hence, they called it the *cosmos*. More popularly, the Greeks believed that the earth arose out of a great void, or emptiness, which they called *chaos*.

Vocabulary

Greek or Latin word	English meaning
aster (ἀστήρ), or astron (ἄστρον)	star
stella, stellae	star
planao (πλανάω)	wander
planetes (πλανήτης) =	
wandering, planet	
sol, solis	sun
helios (ἥλιος)	sun
gala, galactos (γάλα)	milk
cf. lac, lactis = milk	
volvo-volvere-volutum	turn
cosmos (κόσμος)	order
chaos (χάος)	chaos

Signs of the Zodiac (Latin Names)

Aries = Ram	Libra = Scale
Taurus = Bull	Scorpio = Scorpion
Gemini = Twins	Sagittarius = Archer
Cancer = Crab	Capricorn = Goat-horned
Leo = Lion	Aquarius = Water carrier
Virgo = Maiden	Pisces = Fish

THE BIOLOGICAL SCIENCES

Biology is the study of life or living matter in all of its forms. The system of classification of plants and animals that modern biology uses was devised by Carl von Linne (Linnaeus), an 18th-century Swedish scientist who organized the varieties of plants and animals by giving each a double Latin name, the first word denoting the genus, the second, the species.

Vocabulary

Greek or Latin word	English meaning
bios (βίος)	life
genus, generis	birth, origin; offspring; type, kind

cf. genos (γένος) = race, family; offspring; class, kind
species, speciei   form, shape, appearance
  cf. specio-specere = look at; in compounds, -spicio
    specto-spectare-spectatum = watch, observe

Zoology

Zoology is the branch of biology that deals with animals.

Vocabulary

Greek or Latin word	English meaning
zoon (ζῶον)	living thing
cf. -zoon (singular) and -zoa (plural) In compound form used as a suffix in the formation of the names of zoological groups.	
animal, animalis	living being
cf. anima	

Animal	Latin word	Greek word
horse	equus, equi	hippos (ἵππος)
cow	vacca, vaccae	bous (βοῦς) or tauros (ταῦρος)
dog	canis, canis	cyon, cynos (κύων, κυνός)
cat	felis, felis	ailuros (αἴλουρος)
bear	ursa, ursae	arctos (ἄρκτος)
monkey	simia, simiae	pithecos (πίθηκος)

Ornithology

Ornithology is the branch of zoology that deals with the study of birds.

Vocabulary

Greek or Latin word	English meaning
ornis, ornithos (ὄρνις, ὄρνιθος)	bird
avis, avis	bird
pteron (πτερόν)	wing
In compound form, used as a prefix, ptero- = winged	

Entomology

Entomology is the branch of zoology that deals with the study of insects.

Vocabulary

Greek or Latin word	English meaning
entomon (ἔντομον)	notched, cut into pieces
cf. -tomy = cutting	
insectus, insecti	notched, cut into pieces
cf. seco-secare-sectum = cut	
apis, apis = bee	
arachne (ἀράχνη)	spider

An Insect With a Classical Name

According to Greek myth, Arachne was a beautiful young girl who boasted that her spinning was finer than that of the goddess Athene. The two had a contest, and indeed, the work of the mortal girl was better. The goddess flew into a rage and began beating poor Arachne who, in despair, hung herself. Athene took final vengeance by turning her into a spider, but Arachne's talent survived her transformation.

Ichthyology

Ichthyology is the branch of zoology that deals with the study of fish.

Vocabulary

Greek or Latin word	English meaning
ichthys (ἰχθύς)	fish
piscis, piscis	fish
mare, maris	sea

Visual Symbolism

The symbol of the early Christian Church was a fish. This sign was chosen because the Greek word *ichthys* was seen as an acronym for the following words: *Iesu Christos Theou Uios Soter* (Jesus Christ, the Son of God, Savior).

Herpetology

Herpetology is the branch of zoology that deals with the study of reptiles and amphibians.

Vocabulary

Greek or Latin word	English meaning
herpo (ἕρπω)	creep, crawl
serpo-serpere-serptum	creep, crawl
reptilis, reptilis	creeping, crawling; snake
dracon (δράκων)	snake, serpent; dragon

Botany

Botany is the branch of biology that deals with the study of plant life.

Vocabulary

Greek or Latin word	English meaning
botane (βοτάνη)	grass, herb
dendron (δένδρον)	tree
arbor, arboris	tree
phyllon (φύλλον)	leaf
folium, folii	leaf
flos, floris	flower
cf. floreo-florēre = flourish	
radix, radicis	root

Resting on Her Laurels

The Greeks believed that certain places were inhabited by female spirits, called nymphs. Those who liver within trees were called dryads. There are many myths about nymphs, whose numbers were legion, but perhaps the most famous is that of Daphne, who was turned into a laurel tree in order to prevent her capture by the god Apollo, who was pursuing her. The laurel was forever after sacred to Apollo.

Vocabulary

Greek word	English meaning
drys, dryos (δρῦς)	oak tree
daphne (δάφνη)	laurel tree

Genetics

Genetics is that branch of biology which deals with heredity: the transmission of characteristics encoded in the chromosomes of cells from parent to offspring.

Classical mythology records many examples of strange genetic hybrids and mutations: after having had relations with a bull, the Cretan queen Pasiphae gave birth to the Minotaur, a creature with the head of a bull and the body of a man; the Centaurs, who were half horse and half human, were the product of the union between the mortal Ixion and a cloud; Zeus changed himself and Leda into swans so that they might escape the jealous eye of Hera. (Leda subsequently laid an egg out of which hatched four children.)

Modern genetics began much more modestly with the work of Gregor Mendel (1822–1884), an Austrian monk, whose plant-breeding experiments led him to formulate the first principles of heredity. Although his laws have been proven to be not universally true, Mendel's theories on dominant and recessive traits are the basis for today's high-tech genetic engineering. The discovery of DNA and of the techniques of gene manipulation have opened up many possibilities, some perhaps as strange as those described in ancient myths.

Vocabulary

Greek or Latin word	English meaning
genea (γενέα)	family, race
heres, heredis	heir
muto-mutare-mutatum	change
dominor-dominari-dominatum	rule
cf. domus, domus = home	
dominus, domini = master	
hybrida, hybridae*	mixed breed

Note

The molecular form of DNA (deoxyribonucleic acid), present in chromosomes and the carrier of genetic information, has been described as looking like two spirals wound around each other. Check your English dictionary to see how *chromosome* got its name. Can you see which Greek word is its root?

---

*It has been suggested by etymologists that this word is related to the Greek hybris (ὕβρις) = lawless or unnatural action.

Vocabulary

helix ($\H{\eta}\lambda\iota\xi$) = spiral

CHEMISTRY

Modern chemistry and medieval alchemy have the same etymological root,* but their aims are very different. The alchemist sought to transform the "base" metals into gold, thereby transforming himself from a base being into one who was spiritually purified. The goal of alchemy was to discover the "philosopher's stone," or the *elixir vitae*, the substance that all life and matter contained. Although many chemical compounds were discovered and many laboratory instruments that are still being used were invented in this search, the modern science of chemistry asserts that it is much more modest in its goals: it is the study of the compositions and properties of substances and the reactions by which they are produced and changed.

Vocabulary

Greek word	*English meaning*
chemia ($\chi\eta\mu\epsilon\acute{\iota}\alpha$) In compound form, used as a prefix = chemo-	alloying of metals

The Elements

Although modern chemistry defines the term *element* to mean the basic substance that cannot be broken down into simpler ones by chemical means, ancient Greek science held that there were four elements that comprised the cosmos: earth, fire, air, and water.

---

*The medieval Muslim world was very much interested in ancient Greek science and preserved much of that knowledge, which otherwise would have been lost, by translating Greek scientific texts into Arabic. When they found a word that had no Arabic equivalent, they transliterated it and placed the Arabic definite article, *al-*, in front. Hence, alchemy is a hybrid; the article is Arabic, but the base of the word is Greek (see the following). Other scientific terms from Arabic include *elixir*, *alcohol*, and *algebra*.

Vocabulary

Greek or Latin word	English meaning
ge (γῆ)	earth; in compound form, as prefix = geo-
terra, terrae	earth
aer (ἀήρ)	air
aer, aeris	air; in compound form, as prefix = aero-
pyr, pyros (πῦρ)	fire; in compound form, as prefix = pyro-
ignis, ignis	fire
hydor, hydatos (ὕδωρ)	water; in compound form, as prefix = hydro-
aqua, aquae	water

aqua fortis (strong water) = nitric acid

aqua regia (royal water) = nitric and hydrochloric acid

aqua ardens (burning water) = alcohol

aqua vitae (water of life) = alcohol and water. The Gaelic phrase
  for the water of life is *usquebaugh*, which appears in English
  as *whiskey*.

Modern chemistry recognizes over 100 elements; they exist in the form of solid, liquid, or gas. In the periodic table, many elements are represented by the abbreviations of their Latin names.

Vocabulary

Greek or Latin word	English meaning
solidus, solidi	firm; whole, complete
stereos (στερεός)	solid, firm
liquidus, liquidi	liquid
cf. liquor, liqui = flow, melt	
hygros (ὑγρός)	liquid
vapor, vaporis	gas, vapor

Note

The English word *gas* is a learned borrowing coined from the Greek chaos (χάος), meaning void or emptiness.

Some elements with Latin roots	Their Greek equivalents
iron = ferrum, ferri (Fe)	sideros (σίδηρος)
gold = aurum, auri (Au)	chrysos (χρυσός)

copper = cuprum, cupri (Cu)	chalcos (χαλκός)
lead = plumbum, plumbi (Pb)	molybdos (μόλυβδος)
silver = argentum, argenti (Ag)	argyros (ἄργυρος)

Other elements have names that are drawn from Greek and Roman myth:

Promethium = named for Prometheus, who stole fire from the gods and gave it to the human race.

Neptunium = named for Neptune, the Roman god of the sea.

Tantalum = named for Tantalus, who, thinking he could deceive the gods, served them his child, Pelops, in a stew. The divinities were not fooled, and put Pelops back together again.

Plutonium = named for Pluto, a Greek god of the underworld, sometimes associated with Hades.

Selenium = named for Selene, the Greek goddess of the Moon.

Niobium = named for a mortal woman, Niobe, whose many children were killed by Apollo after she boasted of having more children than Leto, the mother of the god. Overwhelmed with grief, she wept unceasingly and was turned to stone.

Biochemistry

Sugar is sweet and so are you...

Biochemistry is that branch of chemistry which deals with living matter. The human body has proved to be a highly sophisticated chemistry lab that is constantly breaking down organic compounds (nutrients) so that they may be used by the body, which produces various enzymes that act as catalysts in this process. During digestion, for example, carbohydrates are converted into glucose, a sugar.

Vocabulary

Greek or Latin word	English meaning
lysis (λύσις)	untying; loosening
zyme (ζύμη)	leaven; yeast; as a learned borrowing, zymo- = leaven
ferveo-fervēre	boil, rage
fermentum, fermenti	leaven, yeast
sacchar (σάκχαρ)	sugar
glycys (γλυκύς)	sweet; as a learned borrowing, glyco- or gluco-
-ose	a learned borrowing used in chemistry to indicate sugar, e.g., maltose, lactose, sucrose, etc.

-ase   a learned borrowing used in chemistry to indi-
                             cate an enzyme, e.g., maltase, lactase, sucrase,
                             etc.

PHYSICS

The modern science of physics deals with the properties, changes, and interactions of matter and energy; but to the ancient Greeks, physics was the inclusive study of natural science or natural philosophy. Modern physics includes the fields of mechanics, optics, and thermodynamics.

Vocabulary

Greek or Latin word	English meaning
ergon (ἔργον)	work
opus, operis	work
labor, laboris	work

Mechanics

Mechanics is that branch of physics that deals with motion and the action of force on bodies.

The modern history of mechanics proves that not all science takes place in the laboratory. According to popular tradition, Galileo investigated the relative speed of falling bodies by dropping objects of differing weights from the top of the Leaning Tower of Pisa; Isaac Newton is said to have been inspired to formulate his theories about the laws of gravity and motion after watching an apple fall from a tree.

Vocabulary

Greek or Latin word	English meaning
moveo-movēre-motum	move
mechane (μηχανή)	machine; contrivance
kinesis (κίνησις)	movement
gravis, gravis	serious; heavy
velox, velocis	swift, rapid

inertia, inertiae   lack of skill; laziness
   cf. ars, artis = skill

Optics

Optics is the branch of physics that deals with the nature and properties of light and vision.

Vocabulary

Greek or Latin word	English meaning
opteuo (ὀπτεύω)	see
phos, photos (φῶς)	light
In compound form, used as a prefix = photo-.	
lux, lucis	light
lumen, luminis	light, source of light
chroma, chromatos (χρῶμα)	color
In compound form, used as a prefix = chromato-.	
pigmentum, pigmenti	color
Also, color, coloris	

Color	Greek	Greek combining form	Latin
white	leucos (λευκός)	leuco-	albus, albi
black	melas (μέλας)	melano-	niger, nigri
red	erythros (ἐρυθρός)	erythro-	ruber, rubri
blue	cyanos (κύανος)	cyano-	caeruleus, caerulei
green	chloros (χλωρός)	chloro-*	viridis, viridis

Thermodynamics

Thermodynamics is the branch of physics that deals with the relationship between heat and energy.

---

*chloro- is also used to indicate the element chlorine, so called because of its greenish-yellow color.

Vocabulary

Greek or Latin word	English meaning
thermos (θεϱμός)	hot, warm
calor, caloris	warmth, heat
dynamis (δύναμις)	power, force
chronos (χϱόνος)	time
tempus, temporis	time
atomos (ἄτομος)	uncut
cf. -otomy, -ectomy	
nucleus, nuclei	kernel
electron (ἤλεκτϱον)	amber
In compound form, used as a prefix	
= electro-	
neuter, neutri	neither

GEOLOGY

Geology is the study of the structure of the earth's crust and the formation of its various layers, including rock types and fossils. In Ancient Greece, the earth was considered to be the oldest of all the deities; her name was Gaia, and she had given birth to the first generation of gods and to all the good things in Nature. We still call our planet Mother Earth.

Vocabulary

Greek or Latin word	English meaning
Ge (Γῆ) or Gaia (Γαῖα)	earth
In compound form, used as a prefix = geo-	
lithos (λίθος)	stone
petros (πέτϱος)	stone, rock
lapis, lapidis	stone
Vulcanus	The Roman blacksmith god who had his forge on Mt. Etna. There he made weapons for the gods and for the heroes.

Paleontology

Paleontology is the branch of geology that deals with prehistoric life through the study of plant and animal fossils (the remains or traces of animal or plant life of an earlier geological age).

Vocabulary

Greek or Latin word	*English meaning*
paleos (παλαιός) In compound form, used as a prefix = paleo-	old
fodio-fodere-fossum	dig up

For the nonspecialist, perhaps the most exciting fossils are those of the dinosaurs, the reptiles who lived during the Mesozoic period (220–65 million years ago). They, too, have a classical name.

Greek word	*English meaning*
dinos (δεινός)	terrible, fearful
sauros (σαῦρος)	lizard

METEOROLOGY

Meteorology is the science that deals with the study of the atmosphere and atmospheric phenomena, including weather and climate.

Vocabulary

Greek or Latin word	*English meaning*
meteoron (μετέωρον)	raised from the ground, high in the air
clima, climatos (κλίμα)	region, zone
atmos (ἀτμός) In compound form, used as a prefix, atmo- = air	vapor
nebula, nebulae	mist, vapor, fog
sphera (σφαῖρα)	ball
nimbus, nimbi In compound form, used as a prefix, nimbo- = cloud	cloud

pluvia, pluviae	rain
glacies, glaciei	ice
baros (βάρος)	weight

In compound form, used as a prefix,
baro- = pressure

Thunder and Lightning

Zeus, of course, was the god who sent thunder and lightning bolts; they were the weapons that he used to show his displeasure and to punish those who had disobeyed him. The Greeks believed that the winds were the children of Eos (Dawn) and Astraeus, a Titan ("the Starry One"):

> Astraeus and Dawn—god and goddess—lay together in love and Dawn gave birth to the violent winds: Zephyr, who brings fair weather, Boreas, who opens a path for the storm, and Notus. After the winds, Dawn gave birth to the stars— the morning star and the shining constellations.
>
> Hesiod, *Theogony* (lines 375–383)

Vocabulary

Greek or Latin word	English meaning
anemos (ἄνεμος)	wind

In compound form, used as a prefix = anemo-

| ventus, venti | wind |

The winds	
Boreas	North Wind
Zephyrus	West Wind
Notus or Auster, Austri	South Wind
Eurus	East Wind
Typhon (Τυφῶν)	a mythological giant

Typhon's body, after he was slain by Zeus, became the source of all harmful winds. He was a dreadful creature, with a hundred fiery serpent heads.

| cyclos (κύκλος) | circle |

In compound words, used as a prefix (cyclo-) or as a suffix (-cycle) = cycle. The winds of a cyclone have circular movement.

The seasons

Latin word	English meaning
aestas, aestatis	summer
autumnus, autumni	fall
tempus hibernum	winter
ver, veris *or* tempus vernum	spring

MATHEMATICS

For the ancient Greeks, mathematics originally was considered to be a branch of philosophy because they believed that through mathematics one could come to

Detail from the arch of Septimius Severus, Roman Emperor (A.D. 193–211).

understand all the physical and spiritual relationships among the constituent parts of the cosmos. Modern mathematics is that branch of knowledge that deals with quantities, magnitudes, and forms, their measurements, and their interrelationships.

Vocabulary

Greek or Latin word	English meaning
manthano (μανθάνω)	learn
Perfect stem = math- (μαθ-)	
mathematica (μαθηματικά)	the things inclined to be learned
arithmos (ἀριθμός)	number
numerus, numeri	number
algebra (Arabic)	reunion, restoration
calculus, calculi	small stone, pebble
gonia (γωνία)	angle
cf. gonu (γόνυ) and genu,	
genus = knee	
q.e.d. = quod erat demonstrandum	that which was to be proved

EXERCISES
(pages 131–138)

In Exercises 1–35 answer each question or fill in the blank(s).

1. An *arbor*etum is a place where _____ are cultivated.

2. A person who enjoys the *piscatorial* art engages in _____.

3. A *herpetologist* is a person who is engaged in _____

   _____.

4. An event of *cosmic* significance affects the _____.

5. *Helio*tropic plants turn toward the _____.

6. A *luna*tic's behavior is supposedly governed by the _____.

7. When we say that the cost of an object is *astro*nomical, we are comparing its cost to the

   _____.

8. Where are we going when we travel *intergalactically*? _____

   _____

9. An *ornithologist* is concerned with the _____   _____.

10. *Deliberation* is the act of _____   _____ a decision.

11. When a disease has been *eradicated*, it has been taken _____ by the
_____.

12. A *portfolio* contains _____ that are _____.

13. *Marine biology* is the _____ of _____ that exists in the
_____.

14. What does a *dendrologist* do? _____   _____

15. A person with a *bovine* appearance resembles a _____.

16. What animal races in a *hippo*drome? _____

17. What characteristics did the *pithecanthropus* possess? _____ and
_____

18. What is the literal meaning of *technocracy*? _____
What is its current meaning? _____

19. A *solarium* is a _____ we can enjoy the _____.

20. What is the literal meaning of *artifice*? _____
What is its current meaning? _____

21. *Lact*ose is a sugar that is present in _____.

22. What is the literal meaning of *cosmopolitan*? _____
What is its current meaning? _____

23. A person who is *circumspect* _____   _____ before
she acts.

24. If we use the word *florid* to describe a person's complexion, what do we mean?
_____

What does *florid* mean if we use it to describe a style of speaking? _____
_____

25. An *omniscient* being _____   _____.

26. *Protozoa* are the _____ forms of _____.

27. The Book of *Genesis* contains an account of the _____ of the world.

28. What is the difference between *etymology* and *entomology*? _____
_____

29. *Innate* characteristics are those that are _____   _____
an individual.

30. What is the literal meaning of *specious*? _____

What is a specious argument? _____

31. If we divide literary works into *genres*, we have classified them according to

    _____ .

32. A *microbe* is a _____ form of _____ .

33. If we *despise* someone, we _____ _____

    that person.

34. A *philodendron* is a plant that is so named because it _____ to

    wrap itself around _____ .

35. Try to discover how the word *genial* came to mean cheerful and pleasant. _____

    _____

(pages 138–147)

In Exercises 36–75 answer each question or fill in the blank(s).

36. A *dyne* is a measure of _____ .

37. A *calorie* is a measure of _____ .

38. A *chronometer* _____ _____ , and is an

    elegant word for a _____ .

39. What metal is found in *ferrous* oxide? _____

40. The French word for money is *argent*. What should it be made of? _____

41. *Chlorophyll* makes the _____ of a plant _____ .

42. If your car's *ignition* really did what its Latin root means, what would happen?

    _____

43. What is a *megalith*? _____ _____ ; what are

    two different meanings of *monolith*? _____

    _____

44. The Roman goddess of the dawn was *Aurora*. What adjective could be used to describe

    her? _____

45. If you are *petrified*, you have been _____ into _____ .

46. A *leuco*cyte is a _____ blood cell.

47. An *aquifer* is a geologic formation that _____ _____ .

48. The *geocentric* theory posited that the _____ was the center of the cosmos.

49. The more common name for an *anemone* is a _____ flower.

50. A *pyromaniac* has a _____ for _____.

51. A *luminary* is a leading _____ in his profession.

52. An *octagon* has _____ _____.

53. A *monochromatic* picture is done in a _____ _____.

54. When you *genu*flect, you bend your _____.

55. *Albumen* is the _____ of an egg.

56. An object that is *translucent* allows _____ to pass _____.

57. What color should a *rubric* be, and what is the present meaning of the word?

_____

58. A *hydr*aulic pump is operated by _____.

59. What is the meaning of the prefix *in-* in the word innumerable? _____

60. The *Paleolithic* period is more commonly known as the _____ _____ Age.

61. If you are diagnosed as being *cyanotic*, you have turned _____.

62. An author's *magnum opus* is her _____ _____.

63. A *polymath* _____ _____ fields.

64. An idea that is *nebu*lous is so vague that it resembles a _____.

65. An object that is *spherical* is shaped like a _____.

66. *Thermal* underwear helps to keep you _____.

67. When is the *vernal* equinox? _____

68. We *hibernate* in the _____; we *estivate* in the _____.

69. What is the literal meaning of *extempore*? _____ _____
    What is its current meaning? _____

70. *Energy* is the capacity to do _____ that is _____ a system.

71. If your teacher gives you a *glacial* stare, he is acting in an _____ manner.

72. What is the literal meaning of *lapidary*? _____
    What do we mean if we say that someone writes in a lapidary style? _____

_____

73. A *photometer* is an _____   _____ .

74. Perhaps one of the most frightening creatures to ever inhabit the earth was the *Tyrannosauros Rex*. What does the name mean? _____

    _____

75. What is the literal meaning of *trigonometry*? _____

    _____

You may get what you ask for

In Exercises 76–80 fill in the blanks with the literal and current meanings of the following words:

	Literal meaning	Current meaning
76. requisition		
77. inquisition		
78. acquisition		
79. perquisite		
80. exquisite		

Plato

Demetrius summoned Stilpo, the philosopher, and asked him whether anyone had robbed him of anything. "No one," said Stilpo, "for I saw no one carrying away knowledge."

PLUTARCH,
The Life of Demetrius

IT'S AN ACADEMIC QUESTION

GREEK EDUCATION

Although students may think that attending school is an occupation as difficult and demanding as any job, and what is more, an absolute necessity for future success, most ancient Greeks and Romans viewed education and learning beyond the basic skills as a luxury available only to those who had money, and therefore the leisure, to devote themselves to study and the pursuit of knowledge.

Vocabulary

Greek or Latin word	English meaning
educo-educare-educatum cf. duco-ducere	train, rear; educate
paedia (παιδεία)	education
	What Greek word forms its root?
schole (σχολή)	leisure
ludus, ludi	sport, game; school
> > > ludo-ludere-lusum	play, make believe, mock
luxuria, luxuriae	extravagance, excess
studeo-studēre	be eager for, be diligent

There were various forms of rudimentary instruction available in classical Athens: reading and writing, poetry and music, and athletics—all for a fee. Al-

153

though they never mandated universal compulsory education, many Greek cities gradually began to supervise education, with the help of wealthy benefactors who provided endowments and paid teachers' salaries. Paedagogy was grounded in memorization and recitation, and discipline was strict.

Vocabulary

Greek or Latin word	*English meaning*
rudis, rudis	rough; unskilled
> > > erudio-erudire-eruditum	polish; educate
struo-struere-structum	build; arrange
mando-mandare-mandatum	order, charge
pello-pellere-pulsum	strike, push
tueor-tuēri-tuitum	look after, guard
cf. tutor, tutoris	guardian, protector
paedagogos (παιδαγωγός)	the slave who accompanied a child to school. The Romans applied the term *paedagogus* more generally to one who taught young children. What are the roots of this word?
disco-discere	learn
> > > discipulus or discipula	pupil
disciplina	instruction, learning
didactos (διδακτός)	taught
doctrina, doctrinae	teaching, instruction
cf. doceo-docēre-doctum	teach, show
magis	more; magis is the comparative adverb of magnus = great
> > > magister, magistri or magistra, magistrae	teacher
examino-examinare-examinatum	weigh, consider

Once the fundamentals had been mastered, it was possible to continue one's education in a variety of subjects. Participation in public life demanded an ability to speak and argue well, and *sophistae*, men who claimed to teach not only the skills of persuasive rhetoric and oratory but also a practical morality, often commanded large fees. Education thus came to be seen as a pragmatic means of producing good citizens and promoting cultural traditions. Not every one approved of the sophists' teaching methods or their goals; Plato's denunciation of this kind of instruction, in which "the weaker argument was made to seem the stronger," gave the name "sophist" the pejorative meaning it has today.

Vocabulary

Greek or Latin word	English meaning
fundus, fundi	bottom, the deep
> > > fundo-fundare-fundatum	lay the bottom; fix, establish
jacio-jacere-jactum	throw, hurl
in compounds, -jicio, -jicere, -jectum	
suadeo-suadēre-suasum	advice, urge
rhetor (ῥήτωρ)	speaker
oro-orare-oratum	speak
sophos (σοφός)	wise, clever
> > > sophistes (σοφιστής)	expert, teacher
pragma, pragmatos (πρᾶγμα)	matter, affair
encomion (ἐγκώμιον)	a speech of praise

At Plato's school, the Academy, and at the Lyceum of Aristotle, advanced instruction was given in the disciplines of philosophy, mathematics, and science. The curriculum of the liberal arts, a product of the approaches of the faculty in these institutions and of the sophists, became the foundation of higher learning in Europe, and formed the basis of the modern college and university. Of course, it wasn't always just hard work; campus life clearly held some pleasures, most notably *symposia*.

Vocabulary

Greek or Latin word	English meaning
encyclios paedia (ἐγκύκλιος παιδεία)	literally, encircling education; general knowledge
curro-currere-cursum	run
> > > curriculum, curriculi	running, race
collegium, collegii	corporation, group
cf. lego-legere-lectum	choose; speak; read
lego (λέγω) has the same meaning	
universitas, universitatis	the whole; community
semen, seminis	seed
> > > seminarium, seminarii	seedbed, nursery
for-fari-fatum	speak
> > > profiteor-profitēri-professum	declare openly, announce
facultas, facultatis	skill, ability
cf. facio-facere	

campus, campi	plain, field
symposion (συμπόσιον)	drinking party

Note

Some Greek and Latin nouns retain their original plural endings in English. Greek words that were adopted by the Romans often have Latin endings in English. For example:

Greek symposion > > > Latin symposium (*sing.*); symposia (*plur.*)
Greek encomion > > > Latin encomium (*sing.*); encomia (*plur.*)
  colloquium (*sing.*); colloquia (*plur.*)

THE LIBERAL ARTS

In the medieval universities of Europe, *the seven liberal arts* were divided into two classes of study: the *quadrivium* and the *trivium*. The *quadrivium* consisted of arithmetic, astronomy, geometry, and music; the *trivium* comprised grammar, rhetoric, and dialectic. What Latin words are at the root of these courses of study?

BOOKS AND LIBRARIES

The first organized research library was said to have been established by Aristotle at the Lyceum, but certainly the largest and most famous library in the ancient world was founded in the third century B.C. at Alexandria in Egypt. It is claimed by contemporary sources that it contained 700,000 volumes. Associated with the library was the Museum, an institute for advanced research under the aegis of the government, where scholars catalogued and edited much of the canon of ancient Greek literature.

The production of books was a difficult and laborious task; each text had to be copied by hand, and errors were inevitable. Most volumes were written on rolls of papyrus, although parchment, made from treated animal skins, was also used. The *codex*, forerunner of the modern book, with bound pages, was not in common use until the 2nd century A.D.

Vocabulary

Greek or Latin word	*English meaning*
liber, libri	book

> > > librarium, librarii	library
biblion (βιβλίον)	book
> > > bibliothece (βιβλιοθήκη)	library
aegis (αἰγίς)	shield
volvo-volvere-volutum	roll
> > > volumen, voluminis	roll, book
papyrus (πάπυρος)	the Egyptian papyrus plant, from whose fiber paper was made
chartes (χάρτης)	papyrus roll
codex, codicis	block of wood; tablet, book
texo-texere-textum	weave
edo-edere-editum	bring forth; publish
canon (κανών)	rule; standard
pinna, pinnae or penna, pennae	feather; wings (*plur.*)

Now, of course, with the widespread use of computers and the electronic transmission, storage, and retrieval of information, printed books may go the way of the feather pen and inkwell. The use of digital computers has introduced a host of new words to the English language, including lots of acronyms, and has given new meaning to old words, such as memory, virtual reality, and flexibility, that are formed from Greek and Latin roots.

Computers may have affected every aspect of modern existence, but like all machines, they have their limitations: wouldn't it be nice if whenever we made an error in our lives, all we had to do was to hit the *cancel* or *delete* key, and erase our mistakes?

Vocabulary

Greek or Latin word	*English meaning*
puto-putare-putatum	consider, think
> > > computo-computare-computatum	sum up, calculate
digitus, digiti	finger, toe
memoria, memoriae	memory
virtus, virtutis	manliness; excellence, worth
flecto-flectere-flexum	change, alter
deleo-delēre-deletum	destroy
erro-errare-erratum	wander, roam

Some computer acronyms

RAM = Random Access Memory
LASER = Light Amplification by Stimulated Emission of Radiation

GIGO = Garbage In, Garbage Out
WYSIWYG = What You See Is What You Get

Notes

Going Around in Circles

Research, the foundation of all good scholarship, is derived from the Latin verb

circo-circare = go around

Stop, Thief!

The root of the word *plagiarism* reveals just how serious a crime it is.

plagio-plagiare-plagiatum = steal, kidnap

Talking may be hazardous to your health

We have already discovered that there are a great many Latin and Greek verbs that mean "to speak." Some of them produce derivative nouns that go beyond plain talking. How many words that have to do with speech can you find in the following sentence? "What fatal pronouncement did the fatuous oracle vocalize when it predicted your future?"

EXERCISES

A. In Exercises 1–42 answer each question or fill in the blank(s).

1. Our il*lusions* help us _____ with reality.
2. A good *educator* should be able to _____ _____ knowledge from her *students*, who are, of course _____ to learn.
3. A person with a *luxuriant* life-style likes _____ in all its forms.
4. A *scholar* needs _____ to do research.
5. The con*struct*ion foreman was in charge of _____ the shopping mall.
6. A person with a *magis*terial manner thinks he has _____ power than others.

7. What are two different meanings of *rude*?

   (a) _____

   (b) _____

8. *Impulse* buying may _____ you _____ owning an item you didn't want or need.

9. A *didactic* person has a desire to _____ when he talks.

10. *Intuition* is a way of _____ _____ a problem.

11. In*doctrin*ation tries to _____ you what to think.

12. An *erudite* individual has come _____ _____ into learning.

13. *Disciplined* study habits enable you to _____.

14. The first question a pragmatist asks is, "What can I _____?"

15. What is a *rhetorical* question? _____

16. *Sophistry* is a _____ form of argument.

17. The speaker delivered an *encomium* to the mayor because he wished to _____ him.

18. A pro*found* statement is one whose meaning is very _____.

19. He let his eye _____ over the newspaper as he gave the headlines a *cursory* glance.

20. When the criminal con*fessed*, he _____ what he had done.

21. What are two different meanings of the word *faculty*?

   (a) _____

   (b) _____

22. A *fatuous* individual tends to _____ without thinking.

23. If you are *elected* to public office, you have been _____ _____ of the field of candidates.

24. If scholars got at the root of *symposium*, they would do a lot more _____ _____ when they got together.

25. Freud was a *seminal* thinker in modern psychology because his work was the _____ _____ for all future investigation.

26. *Illegible* writing is _____ _____ _____.

27. When my friend said he planned to travel *via* public transportation, I knew he planned to come _____ the bus or train.

28. When Roman law was *codified*, it was _____ into a

    _____ .

29. What are the Spanish and French words for library?

    (a) _____

    (b) _____

30. Non*canon*ical works are those that lie outside the _____ of
    what is acceptable.

31. A *pennant* is a banner or flag whose shape resembles a _____ .

32. His sentences were so con*voluted* that they _____ inside each other.

33. Your re*putat*ion reveals what others _____ about you.

34. A statement made in con*text* must be _____ into
    the larger picture.

35. How high can you count if you use all your *digits*? _____

36. He was such a *repulsive* individual that his behavior _____ every-
    one _____ .

37. The *deleterious* effect of drugs can _____ you.

38. What are *memorabilia*? _____

39. We all wish we had *tutelary* spirits who would _____ us from harm.

40. He had only a *rudimentary* education, so he was _____ in reading.

41. When the judge ordered him to be *remanded* into custody, he knew that he had been

    _____ _____ to jail.

42. A *fabulous* party is worth _____ about.

B. *How many ways can you throw*? What is the literal meaning of each of the following
words (43–47); what is its current meaning?

English word	Literal meaning	Current meaning
43. rejection	_____	_____
44. conjecture	_____	_____
45. subjective	_____	_____
46. abject	_____	_____
47. projectile	_____	_____

C. Here are more words, some of them quite elegant, that come into English unchanged from either Greek or Latin. Use your unabridged dictionary to discover the original and current meanings of the following words (48–61):

English word	Greek or Latin meaning	Current meaning
48. opprobrium		
49. veto		
50. eureka		
51. kudos		
52. memento		
53. scintilla		
54. lacuna		
55. enigma		
56. stigma		
57. errata		
58. item		
59. verbatim		
60. hiatus		
61. interim		

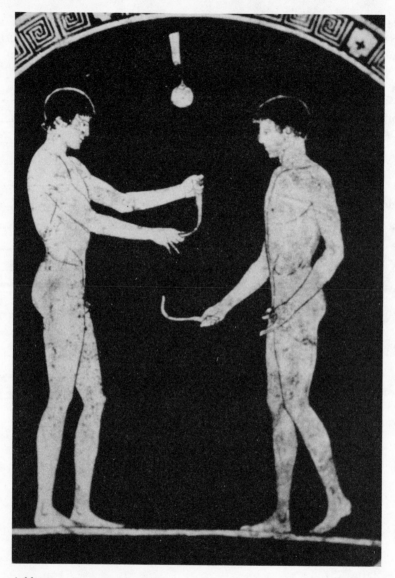

Athletes

We (Athenians) cultivate a taste for the beautiful with moderation and we love knowledge without softness.

Pericles' Funeral Oration (430 B.C.)

THE CLASSICAL INFLUENCE

Western European culture has seen itself as the intellectual heir, in both form and content, of the artistic traditions of Greece and Rome. Although a great variety of non-European cultural forces have also had an impact on the development of Western thought, many of the European traditions of creative expression, from the plastic and decorative arts to architecture to literature, can trace their ancestry back to the monumental legacy of the civilizations of the classical world.

THE FINE ARTS

The Greek exploration of spiritual and intellectual expression through the plastic arts established the forms and styles that were to become the reference points for all subsequent activity in these creative fields in classical antiquity. It was an influence that survived the end of the classical world; the European fascination with the human form, especially as expressed in sculpture, as well as the ideals of harmony and proportion, which provide the basis of classical architecture, perhaps have their origins in the Greek search for rationality, order, and measure in the visible world, as depicted through the various modes of their artistic expression.

Vocabulary

Greek or Latin word	*English meaning*
colo-colere-cultum	inhabit, dwell

> > > colonia, coloniae	estate; settlement
heres, heredis	heir; possessor; successor
plasticos (πλαστικός)	molded
decus, decoris	ornament, splendor, honor
creo-creare-creatum	bring forth, make
> > > cresco-crescere-cretum	arise, become visible
harmonia (ἁρμονία)	fitting together; joining; harmony
monumentum, monumenti	monument
cf. moneo-monēre-monitum	warn
sculpo-sculpere-sculptum	form, fashion
ordo, ordinis	rank, order
pingo-pingere-pictum	represent, paint
architectura, architecturae	the art of building. Although this is a Latin word, what reveals its Greek origin?
ratio, rationis	plan; thought; order

Note

The term *classical* is the term usually applied to Greek art of the fifth and fourth centuries B.C. More generally, it is used to describe the civilization of Greek and Roman antiquity, and has come to represent a particular artistic or architectural style modelled on Greek and Roman prototypes.

classis = type, class
> > > classicus = belonging to a class; belonging to the highest class

Pots and Pans

Greek pottery was valued both for its utility and its beauty. Often elaborately decorated with scenes or figures from Greek myth, these products, ranging from storage jars to drinking cups, found their way all around the Mediterranean world.

Vocabulary

Greek or Latin word	*English meaning*
ceramia (κεραμεία)	pottery
amphoreus (ἀμφορεύς)	two-handled storage jar
crater (κρατήρ)	mixing bowl
labor, laborari, laboratum	work

CITY PLANNING

The Romans, whose aesthetic tastes were in part influenced by Greek models, were innovators as well, especially in the realm of both public and private architecture and city planning. In order to unite the various provinces of an empire that extended from Britain to Mesopotamia, from the Danube to North Africa, Rome built a remarkable system of roads whose remains can be seen even today.

Vocabulary

Greek or Latin word	*English meaning*
urbs, urbis	city
municipium, municipii	town
porta, portae	city gate
vicinia, viciniae	neighborhood
aedificium, aedificii	building. What Latin verb can you see in this word?
domus, domi	house
tego-tegere-tectum	cover
> > > tectum, tecti	roof; building
villa, villae	farmhouse
fenestra, fenestrae	window
murus, muri	wall
atrium, atrii	entry hall
cella, cellae	small room
camera, camerae	vault; private room
cubo-cubare-cubitum	lie down
in compounds, this often appears as -cumbo, -cumbere, -cubitum	
cubiculum, cubiculi	bedroom
forum, fori	outside space; marketplace; place of assembly
agora (ἀγορά)	marketplace; place of assembly
Palatium, Palatii	one of the seven hills of Rome, on which the Emperor Augustus built his residence
circus, circi	circle
iter, itineris	path, route; journey
via, viae	path, street, way

Note

Although Christianity took root relatively quickly in the various cities and urban centers of the Roman Empire, there were many Romans, especially in the outlying districts, who held on to their traditional ways long after Christianity was recognized as the official Roman religion in the 4th century A.D.

The poet Sappho

Vocabulary

Greek or Latin word	English meaning
pagus, pagi	country district
> > > paganus, pagani	rural
rus, ruris	countryside

LITERATURE

The ancient Greeks created enduring models for many of the genres of later European literature. Poetry in its various forms, as well as comedy, tragedy, and historiography—all can trace their roots to the classical literary traditions.

Vocabulary

Greek or Latin word	English meaning
littera, litterae	letter; literature (*plur.*)
poietes (ποιητής)	maker, poet
cf. poeta, poetae	poet
hymnos (ὕμνος)	a song in praise of a deity
paean (παιάν)	a song of thanksgiving to Apollo, the god of healing
drama (δρᾶμα)	doing
historia (ἱστορία)	inquiry

THEATER

Although its exact origins are a matter of debate, it is clear that Greek theater had its beginnings in religious ritual; tragedies and comedies were performed at public festivals in honor of Dionysus, the god of wine and fertility, who promised his worshippers release from the bonds of ordinary life. The Greek philosopher Aristotle, in trying to define tragedy, said that it was the representation of an action that, by means of arousing "pity and fear," attempted to purge these emotions.

The production of the tragedies, which drew their themes and plots, for the most part, from Greek myth, was part of a competition subsidized by the state; the wealthiest citizens paid the costs, including the training of the dramatic chorus, as a civic obligation. The judges, who were chosen by lot in order to prevent bribery, seem to have based their awards on audience applause.

In its most developed form, the cast consisted of three actors (female roles were played by men) and the members of the chorus. Originally, the author also acted in the production of his work; eventually, the state provided the leading actor. The playwright Sophocles, author of *Oedipus* and *Antigone*, is said to have been a skilled musician and graceful dancer who performed in several of his own works.

Not all Greek theater was serious and solemn. Comedy, with its sometimes fantastic plots, took pleasure in being raucous and often lewd, and in poking fun at popular religious beliefs, social relationships, as well as prominent Athenian citizens, politicians, artists, and intellectuals.

Vocabulary

Greek or Latin word	English meaning
theao (θεάω)	look at, see
> > > theatron (θέατρον)	theater
tragoedia (τραγῳδία)	literally, goat-song; tragedy
comos (κῶμος)	revel; merry-making
> > > comoedia (κωμῳδία)	comedy
mimesis (μίμησις)	representation; imitation
catharsis (κάθαρσις)	cleansing; purification
character (χαρακτήρ)	mark, stamp; special type
crino (κρίνω)	judge
> > > crisis (κρίσις)	decision; trial; dispute
> > > criticos (κριτικός)	able to judge
hypocrites (ὑποκριτής)	actor
choreuo (χορεύω)	dance in a circle
augeo-augēre-auctum	increase; enrich
agon (ἀγών)	contest, struggle
protagonistes (πρωταγωνιστής)	leading actor
clamo-clamare-clamatum	call out, shout
plaudo-plaudere-plausum	clap, strike
in compounds, -plodo-plodere-plosum	

Greek theater has proved to be a lasting influence, not only as a literary form, but architecturally as well.

Vocabulary

Greek word	English meaning
scene (σκηνή)	tent; stage backdrop
orchestra (ὀρχήστρα)	place where the chorus danced

Note

The shout of *encore,* meaning more or again, is derived from the Latin phrase *in hanc horam* = at this time; still, yet.

The Muses

Traditionally, every artist claimed that he was inspired by the Muses, the divine daughters of Zeus and the goddess Memory. The nine sisters each had a particular sphere of creative activity over which she presided.

Mnemosyne = Memory
Calliope = Muse of epic poetry
Clio = Muse of history
Erato = Muse of lyric poetry
Euterpe = Muse of flute playing
Melpomene = Muse of tragedy
Polyhymnia = Muse of sacred song
Terpsichore = Muse of dance
Thalia = Muse of comedy
Urania = Muse of astronomy

Vocabulary

Greek or Latin word	English meaning
spiro-spirare-spiratum	breathe
musice (μουσική)	belonging to the Muses

MUSIC

Much of musical terminology and many musical instruments—woodwinds, strings, and percussion—have classical roots.

Vocabulary

Greek or Latin word	English meaning
sono-sonare-sonitum	sound
melodia (μελῳδία)	song

canto-cantare-cantatus	sing
organon (ὄργανον)	instrument
stringo-stringere-strictum	draw tight; bind; cut off
percutio-percutere-percussum	strike
cornu, cornus	horn
xylon (ξύλον)	wood
clarus, clari	clear
cymbalon (κύμβαλον)	cymbal
tympanon (τύμπανον)	drum
cithara (κιθάρα)	lyre, lute

Note

From A to Z: The first note on the musical scale in the medieval period was designated by the Greek letter *gamma*, whereas the final note was called *ut*. Thus, the word *gamut*, a contraction of *gamma* and *ut*, was used to denote the entire scale of tones. Today, the word is used to mean the entire range of any area, as in the phrase, "his emotions ran the gamut from grief to anger."

ATHLETES, COMPETITION, AND EXCELLENCE

Theater was not the only form of leisure entertainment available to the Greeks and Romans, and the competitive spirit extended into the realm of physical activity. Wrestling, jumping, discus and javelin throwing, and running were all part of public contests sponsored by the state or by wealthy individuals. Heracles, that Greek hero known for his remarkable strength, was credited with founding the Olympic games; and although they were dedicated to Zeus, the contests in the stadium provided an arena for the demonstration of human excellence. The entrants competed on behalf of their cities, and victors often received the same kind of public prestige (and rewards) as modern athletes.

Sometimes, the original purpose of the contest seems to have been lost. Roman gladiatorial combat, for example, probably had begun as part of funeral ritual, but by the imperial period, sponsorship of these violent spectacles had become merely a means for politicians to win popular support and to keep the populace happy.

Vocabulary

Greek or Latin word	*English meaning*
athlos (ἆθλος)	contest

sthenos (σθένος)	strength
peto-petere-petitum	seek, strive
gymnazo (γυμνάζω)	exercise, train
discos (δίσκος)	plate, disc
stadion (στάδιον)	racecourse
dromos (δρόμος)	running
praestigiae, praestigiarum	delusion, deception. Check your unabridged dictionary to see how the word *prestige* took on a positive meaning.
arena, arenae	sand; arena
gladius, gladii	sword
pugno-pugnare-pugnatum	fight
spectro-spectare-spectatum	look at
> > > spectaculum, spectaculi	spectacle
testor-testari-testatum	show, prove; witness

Note

leisure, the freedom from activity, is legal.

   cf. licet = it is permitted

Setting a Record

According to Greek tradition, when the Athenians defeated the Persians at the Battle of Marathon in 490 B.C., the runner Pheidippides raced the 26 miles back to Athens to announce the good news. *Marathon* now denotes any long race, whereas the ending *-thon* has been used to coin many words, all having the sense of endurance—e.g., telethon and walkathon.

Approval Ratings

When a fighter fell in the arena, the spectators often expressed their feelings: traditionally, the gesture of *thumbs up* indicated that the gladiator should be spared by his opponent; *thumbs down* indicated that the victor should show no mercy. The Roman satirist Juvenal declared that the citizens of Rome had become so decadent that they cared only for *panem et circenses*, "bread and circuses," that is, free food and public entertainment, provided by politicians eager to buy votes.

Vocabulary

Latin word	English meaning
vinco-vincere-victum	conquer
cado-cadere-casum	fall
in compounds, -cido, -cidere, -cisum	
votum, voti	vow, oath
ambitio, ambitionis	going around; canvassing for votes; desire for office

Some New Beginnings

You have already learned (p. 35) that -sco indicates what is called an inceptive verb, meaning that the action has just begun, or is continuing. Here are a few more verbs that belong to this category:

Inceptive Latin verb	English meaning
effervesco, effervescere	boil up, foam
adolesco, adolescere, adultum	grow up
coalesco, coalescere, coalitum	grow together, become one
obsolesco, obsolescere, obsoletum	wear out

EXERCISES

In Exercises 1–63 answer each question or fill in the blanks.

A. *Fine Arts and City Planning*

1. A *dom*esticated animal should be able to live in your _____.

2. By looking at the *itiner*ary, I knew which _____ he had taken.

3. What is the difference in meaning between *urban* and *urbane*? _____

   _____

4. *Ordin*al numbers are used to place a series in _____.

5. What is the shape of London's Picadilly *Circus*? _____

6. I don't know why my boss was so angry when she found me napping in my *cubicle*; after all, it was designed for _____.

7. *Deviant* behavior goes _____ _____.

8. What activity went on in the Roman *Forum* that gives the word its present meaning?
_____

9. When he threatened to de*fenestrate* me, I moved away from the _____.

10. The *detect*ive solved the crime by taking _____ its _____.

11. What are two different meanings of *cultivated*?

    (a) _____

    (b) _____

12. As I saw the *portals* close, I knew I'd never get beyond those _____.

13. If you undergo *plastic* surgery, you will have some part of your anatomy _____
_____.

14. *Municipal* officials are in charge of _____.

15. When a writer *depicts* a character, he makes a _____
_____ it.

16. What is a *protege* and what is its literal meaning? From what language did it enter into
English? _____
_____

17. I went to see the *murals* he had painted in his house, but they had torn down the _____
_____.

18. What are the meanings of *edification* and *edifice*?

    (a) _____

    (b) _____

19. *Recreat*ional activities should _____ life in us _____.

20. When the police officer said that the criminal was in the *vicinity*, where was the evil-
doer? _____

21. A *village* should contain _____.

22. I was pleased when my boss told me I would get an *increment* because that meant my
take-home pay would _____.

23. When she presented her *rationale* for acting in this way, I understood her _____
_____.

24. If your teacher *admonishes* you, she is making a _____
_____ you.

25. What are two different meanings of *incumbent*?

    (a) _____

    (b) _____

26. The legislative branch of the U.S. government is *bicameral*. What does that mean?
_____

27. The farmhouse had a *rustic* charm that can be found only in the _____ .

28. Their *collaboration* was a failure because they were unable to _____
    well _____ .

29. What is the connection between *increase* and *crescent*? _____
    _____ What is the current meaning of each word?
    _____

B. *Literature, Theatre, Music*

30. It was clear that he had won *plaudits* for his performance because everyone was _____
    _____ .

31. His *theatri*cal performance was truly something to _____ .

32. *Illicit* behavior is _____ _____ .

33. A *literal*-minded person takes at face value every _____ she reads.

34. Everyone's *character* has its own particular _____ .

35. The *choreographer* _____ _____ for a
    performance.

36. What is the literal meaning of *conspirator*? _____

37. When I heard the *clamor* in the street, I looked to see who was _____ .

38. The students' *petition* _____ the abolition of all home-
    work.

39. He took a second job to *aug*ment his wages because he needed to _____
    his salary.

40. We had reached a *crisis*; it was time to make a _____ .

41. Paying his debts was a *cathartic* experience, because it _____
    him of guilt.

42. I knew he was a *hypocrite*, only _____ that he was sorry.

43. When the witness *attested* to the evidence, he _____
    _____ its truth.

44. *Cliometrics* is that branch of the study of _____ that
    attempts to _____ various economic or social facts.

45. A *plaus*ible idea is one that is worthy of _____ .

46. If *orchestra* had kept its original meaning, what would be going on there? _____

_____ .

47. A *mnemonic* device helps you _____ something.

48. *Critics* are supposed to be able to _____ works of art.

49. I suffered a con*cussion* when I was _____ on the head.

50. *Cornucopia* is an elegant word for a _____ .

51. A *cantata* is a musical composition that is meant to be _____ .

52. I took *drastic* measures because it was clearly necessary to _____ something.

53. As she *agonized* over her exam, I could see that it was a _____ .

C. *Athletics and Contests*

54. People should _____ in a *gymnasium*.

55. Calli*sthenics* is a way of giving your body _____ .

56. A remark that *impugns* your reputation _____ _____ _____ it.

57. She entered the *pentathlon* even though she wasn't sure she could finish all _____

_____ .

58. He was a *casual* person; he took things as they _____ .

59. An *invincible* enemy is one who is _____ _____ _____ .

60. A *pugn*acious individual is always looking for a _____ .

61. My friends gave me a *testimonial* dinner as _____ of my success.

62. Why is the West called the *Occident*? _____

63. Her deeply held con*vict*ions _____ all their doubts.

Detail from a bronze of Zeus, ruler of the Greek gods. (Some scholars have identified this statue as Poseidon.)

Homer and Hesiod have attributed to the gods all things that are a shame and a reproach among men: stealing and adultery and deceiving one another.

XENOPHANES (6TH CENTURY B.C. PHILOSOPHER)

MYTH, RELIGION, AND PHILOSOPHY

The traditional religion of the Greeks and Romans was polytheistic in structure; and the Greeks and Romans loved to tell stories about all their gods and goddesses: what they looked like, how they behaved, whom among the mortals and other deities they loved or hated. Although the religious practices and beliefs of the Greeks and Romans eventually disappeared, the stories of their gods and heroes contained in classical literature became one of the most important foundation stones of European cultural traditions. The themes of Greek and Roman myth have been utilized over and over again in literature, art, and music, while the names and exploits of the various gods, fabulous creatures, and mortal heroes and heroines still live on in our language.

Vocabulary

Greek or Latin word	English meaning
religio, religionis	religion
perhaps derived from	
ligo-ligare-ligatum = bind	
theos (θεός)	god
deus, dei	god
divus, divi	god, divine
mythos (μῦθος)	story
fabula, fabulae	story

THE GREEK AND ROMAN GODS

Just as there are similarities between the Greek and Latin languages because they both belong to the Indo-European family and thus have a common ancestry, there are also similarities between the pantheons of their gods for the very same reason. In addition, the Romans adapted and retold many Greek myths for their own use, so that often a hero will have both a Greek and a Latin name, e.g., Odysseus (Greek) who was called Ulysses by the Romans. Because Roman culture had a more direct influence on Western tradition than did Greek, the names of the Roman deities are perhaps more familiar to us.

The Greek Gods and Their Roman Counterparts

Greek god	Roman god	Function
Zeus	Jupiter (Jove)	ruler of the gods and mortals
Hera	Juno	wife and consort of Zeus (Jove); patron of marriage and the family
Poseidon	Neptune	ruler of the sea
Demeter	Ceres	goddess of grain and fertility
Athene	Minerva	goddess of wisdom; patron of arts and crafts; protector of heroes
Artemis	Diana	goddess of the hunt; protector of wild things; guardian of children
Ares	Mars	god of war and destruction
Aphrodite	Venus	goddess of sexual passion and fertility
Hades, Plutus	Saturnus, Pluto	god of the underworld
Hermes	Mercury	messenger of the gods
Hephaestus	Vulcan	blacksmith and fire god
Apollo*		god of light and inspiration; patron of the arts
Titans*		race of giants who ruled the world before Zeus
Atlas*		Titan who held the sky on his shoulders
Prometheus*		Titan who sided with Zeus and who later stole fire from the gods to give to man
Dionysus (Bacchus)*		god of wine and flowing fertility
Pan*		god of shepherds and flocks, often associated with Dionysus
Muses*		the nine goddesses who gave inspiration to those who were creative in the arts

*The Romans called these deities by their Greek names.

Venus de Milo. 3rd century B.C. statue of the goddess Venus
(Aphrodite), discovered on the island of Melos and now in the Louvre.

Greek god	Function
Nemesis*	goddess of retribution
Moirae*	the three Fates: Clotho (the Spinner); Lachesis (the Measurer); and Atropos (the Cutter)

*Nemesis and Moirae have no direct Latin equivalents.

THE CALENDAR

The English names of the months of the year that we use today are derived from their Latin names, although the Roman calendar was structured somewhat differently from ours.

Vocabulary

Greek or Latin word	English meaning
dies, diei	day
hemera ($\dot\eta\mu\acute\epsilon\varrho\alpha$)	day
mensis, mensis	month
annus, anni	year

The Months

January, named for Janus, the two-faced god of doorways, gates, and beginnings
February, named for *Februa*, a Roman feast of purification held during that month
March, named for Mars
April, from the Latin verb *aperio* = open, because this is a time when the earth begins to bloom
May, named for Maia, a goddess of fertility
June, named for Juno
July, named for Julius Caesar
August, named for Augustus Caesar
September, October, November, and December are, of course, derived from Roman numbers. How many months, then, did the Roman calendar originally have?

The Calends was the first day of the Roman month. Since monthly interest was calculated by the *Calends*, an account ledger was called a *calendarium*. The only other days of the month noted by the Romans were the *Nones* (the 5th of the month, except in March, May, July, and October when it fell on the 7th) and the *Ides* (the 13th, except in March, May, July, and October when it fell on the 15th). It was not until quite late that the Romans adopted the practice of naming days in a repetitive cycle.

The English names of the days of the week are derived from the gods of Germanic myth.

OTHER TIMES...

hora, horae	hour
ante meridiem	before the middle of the day
post meridiem	after the middle of the day
cras	tomorrow
aeon (αἰών)	an age; a long period of time
aevum, aevi	a period of time; an age
saeculum, saeculi	generation; spirit of an age

OTHER PLACES...

Greek myth describes an often fabulous world, and that landscape has also become part of our vocabulary.

Mount Olympus: residence of many of the Greek gods, who were thus referred to as the Olympians.

Styx: the main river in the underworld and also its boundary line. The ancient Greeks believed that in order to enter the realm of Hades, one had to be ferried across the Styx by the boatman Charon, at the cost of one obol; thus, the dead were buried with a coin in their mouths. The adjective "stygian" is used to describe a place that is dark and gloomy.

Lethe: river in the underworld whose water caused the dead to forget their past lives.

Elysium or *Elysian Fields*: the dwelling place of those few lucky mortals who had been granted eternal conscious life and happiness by the gods.

Augean stables: the stables of King Augeas were so filthy that the Greek hero Heracles, as one of his labors, had to divert two rivers in order to cleanse them in a single day.

Labyrinth: a maze built on Crete for King Minos by the famed Greek architect Daedalus, in order to keep imprisoned the Minotaur, a man-eating creature that was half-bull and half-human.

MYTHIC CREATURES

The human imagination is a wonderful creative force, and many of the mythic monsters continue to haunt us:

Sphinx: a winged female monster who would eat young men who could not answer her riddle, "What walks on four legs in the morning, two legs in the afternoon, and three legs in the evening?" She committed suicide when Oedipus gave the correct answer.

Medusa: one of the three monstrous Gorgons, she had hair of snakes; her glance turned men into stone. She was slain by the hero Perseus.

Chimera: a fire-breathing monster who had the head of a lion, the torso of a goat, and the tail of a snake. The adjective "chimerical" is used to describe something that is wildly fanciful or unrealistic.

Sirens: bird-like women who lured sailors to their deaths by singing sweet and entrancing melodies while sitting on the treacherous rocks that rose up from the sea.

Harpies: bird-like women who tormented a variety of people in Greek myth by snatching away food from those who were hungry.

Phoenix: a fabulous bird of great beauty, said to live for 500 years, after which it would immolate itself on a pyre, and then rise up once again, reborn, from the ashes.

Gryphon or Griffin: a mythic creature with the head and wings of an eagle and the body of a lion.

Other myths have become part of our common cultural vocabulary, for constant allusion is still made to the stories of:

Pandora's Box. Pandora, the first woman, who was created by the gods as revenge for Prometheus' theft of fire, was given a box containing all the evils in the world. Instructed not to open it, she disobeyed and released every kind of suffering into the world. Only Hope remained inside.

King Midas and his Golden Touch. Because he had done a kindness to the god Dionysus, Midas was granted any wish he might desire. Requesting that everything he touch turn to gold, he was at first delighted with his gift, but soon begged the god to take back his gift. He had turned his daughter into gold, and he was starving to death as well. Although the gift of the golden touch proved to be disastrous, we now often use the term in a positive way.

The Amazons. The Amazons were said to be a race of warrior women who lived without men, and who excelled at those activities, such as hunting and fighting, normally thought to belong to the male sphere.

Proteus. Proteus was a god of the sea who, like the water, could change himself into whatever form he wished. The English adjective, *protean*, which means extremely variable, is derived from his name.

The Labors of Hercules. Hercules (or, as the Greeks called him, Heracles) was the greatest of the ancient mythological heroes. In order to gain immortal glory, he had to perform twelve death-defying labors, including a journey to the Underworld.

The Golden Fleece. The Greek hero Jason was sent on a meant-to-be fatal quest to retrieve the golden fleece of a ram. The fleece was guarded by a fire-breathing dragon who never slept; but Jason, with the help of the witch Medea, was able to steal the skin and escape.

Procrustes. Procrustes was said to have entertained his guests by inviting them to spend the night. If they did not fit exactly into the bed he offered, Procrustes would either stretch them or lop off their heads to insure a perfect night's sleep. The English adjective, *procrustean*, is used to describe arbitrary and violent means of insuring conformity.

Sisyphus. For some unspecified crime, Sisyphus was condemned by the gods to forever push a boulder to the top of a hill in the Underworld, only to watch it roll back down once again. His name has become synonomous with futility.

TROY

Perhaps the best known and most influential of all the Greek myths is the cycle of stories that have to do with the Trojan War, a ten-year struggle waged between the city of Troy and the Greek forces over the beautiful Helen, who had a face "that launched a thousand ships." Writers and artists through the ages have continued to draw upon the characters and events that the Greek poet Homer first described in the *Iliad* and *Odyssey* more than 2700 years ago.

The Trojan War

These names that figure prominently in the story of Troy are still part of our imaginative vocabulary:

Apple of Discord. Eris, the goddess of Strife, angered at not being invited to the wedding of Peleus and Thetis, threw a golden apple inscribed with the words "to the fairest," among the divine guests. Athene, Hera, and Aphrodite all laid claim.

The Judgment of Paris. Zeus, wisely deciding not to get involved, chose Paris, a young Trojan prince, to judge the beauty contest among the goddesses. Each offered him a bribe, but Paris selected Aphrodite because she promised him Helen.

Helen. Helen was Paris' prize, but unfortunately, she was married to Menelaus, a Greek king. It was the kidnapping of Helen that led to the outbreak of the war.

Achilles. Achilles, son of the mortal Peleus and the goddess Thetis, was the greatest of the Greek heroes to fight at Troy. According to at least one tradition, his mother dipped him in the river Styx in order to make him invulnerable; unfortunately, she was holding him by the heel, where he remained vulnerable.

Myrmidons. The Myrmidons were the loyal group of Achilles' followers who accompanied the hero to Troy. The name is now applied to anyone who blindly follows the commands of his leader.

Hector. In the *Iliad*, Hector is the gallant leader of the Trojan forces; but later traditions depicted him as a domineering bully. Thus, we have the English verb *hector*, which means to act in an overbearing way.

Priam begging Achilles for the body of Hector.

Cassandra. Cassandra, the daughter of the king of Troy, had been given the gift of prophecy by Apollo, who had hoped to win her love. When she spurned him, however, the god caused her not to be believed. She foresaw the destruction of her city, but her visions were ignored. The name is now applied to anyone who predicts doom and disaster.

Trojan Horse. After ten years of fighting, the Greeks still had not taken Troy, for the city had strong and well-defended walls. It was only through the deceit by means of the huge wooden horse, whose belly was filled with Greek soldiers, that the Greeks were able to gain entry and thus capture Troy. The name is now applied to anyone or anything that seeks to destroy from within.

Stentor. Stentor was the herald of the Greek army, whose voice was as loud as those of fifty men. The adjective *stentorian* is now applied to a person having a very loud and powerful voice.

Odysseus. Odysseus was a good fighter at Troy, but his adventures really began on his journey back to his native Ithaca, a trip which took him nine years. Despite all his spectacular experiences, recorded in the *Odyssey*, all that Odysseus could dream of was returning home.

Penelope. While Odysseus wandered, Penelope, his faithful wife, kept off the advances of many suitors who wished not only to marry her, but to gain Odysseus' kingdom. By a variety of clever stratagems, she fended them off until Odysseus' return.

Circe. On their return voyage, Odysseus and his men landed on the island of Aeaea, the residence of Circe. Circe's powers of enchantment were so strong that she could change humans into animal form.

Calypso. Calypso was a goddess who lived on the island of Ogygia. She fell so deeply in love with Odysseus when he was washed up on the island that she offered him the gift of immortality if he would live there with her forever. Although Odysseus remained with Calypso for seven years, he yearned only for his home and for Penelope.

Mentor. Mentor, a friend of Odysseus, gave helpful advice and protection to Odysseus' son, Telemachus, while Odysseus was absent. The word is now used for a wise counselor or teacher.

The story of the Trojan War and of the aftermath of the city's destruction was retold by the Roman poet Vergil in his epic, the *Aeneid*. The Romans traditionally believed that they were the descendants of those few brave Trojan survivors, led by the hero Aeneas, who made their way out of the burning city. This work, modeled on both the *Iliad* and the *Odyssey*, contains many notable lines of Latin verse, and among the most famous are these:

Quidquid id est, timeo Danaos et dona ferentis
  "Whatever it is, I fear the Greeks, even those bearing gifts."

Varium et mutabile semper femina
  "A woman is a fickle and changeable thing."

ANCIENT PEOPLE AND PLACES

Figures from Greek and Roman history and real places in the ancient world have also found their way into the English vocabulary.
  What do the following terms mean now and what were their origins?

Pyrrhic victory	spartan
philippic	laconic
mausoleum	arcadian
draconian	solecism
"rich as Croesus"	sybaritic

PHILOSOPHY

Philosophy is literally the "love of wisdom," but for the Greeks, philosophy had as its original impetus the search for the causes of things, both physical and ethical. The earliest Greek philosophers, who were called physicists, were concerned with the nature and constituent parts of the physical cosmos, and the relationship between the world of nature and the world of human activity. The focus of later Greek and Roman philosophy, however, was the realm of human action, behavior, and spiritual goals: how are we to act best in this world? What is the best form of polity? Is it possible to achieve happiness? Is the human soul immortal? The various schools of ancient philosophy still find expression today, not only in the questions they raised and the ideals they pursued, but in their language and forms of argumentation as well.

Socrates

Vocabulary

Greek or Latin word	English meaning
sophia (σοφία)	wisdom
ethos (ἦθος)	custom, usage; character, disposition
mos, moris	manner, custom, usage
ingenium, ingenii	natural quality, inborn characteristic
cf. genus, generis	

platonic: pertaining to the theories of the 4th-century B.C. Greek philosopher Plato, and most often used now to refer to his elevation above all else of a spiritual love untouched by physical desire.

academic: pertaining to the Academy, the school founded by Plato; the word is most commonly used now to mean scholarly or learned, but without practical usefulness.

stoic: pertaining to the ideas of the school of philosophy founded in the fourth century B.C. by Zeno; the word is most often used today to refer one of the central doctrines of the school, that we should submit uncomplainingly to Fate, and "go with the flow." The word is derived from *stoa* (στοά), a detached portico where Zeno supposedly did his teaching.

epicurean: pertaining to the teachings of the Greek philosopher Epicurus, who preached that the highest good is pleasure, which his followers interpreted as freedom from pain or disturbance, but which his critics took as unbridled freedom and self-indulgence. The word is now used to refer to the enjoyment of sensual pleasures, especially in eating and drinking.

hedonism: the doctrine that teaches that pleasure or happiness is the highest good. The word is derived from *hedone* (ἡδονή) = pleasure.

cynic: pertaining to the ideas of a school of Greek philosophy that preached independence of action and freedom from societal conventions. The etymology of the name is a matter of debate; the root of the word is *kyon* (κύων = dog), and it has been suggested that the word derived from the fact that the Cynics were noted for their rather rude behavior. The Cynics went out of their way to violate social norms; perhaps the most famous of the Cynics was Diogenes, who went about with a lantern, saying that he was looking for an honest man. Today the word is used to describe someone who questions social values and distrusts human sincerity and moral purpose.

Forms of Philosophical and Logical Argumentation

Latin phrase	Literal meaning	Current meaning
a fortiori	from the stronger	for a still stronger reason
a posteriori	from the one after	from effect to cause; based on observation or experience
a priori	from the one before	from cause to effect; valid independent of experience

ad hoc	to this thing	for a special purpose
ad hominem	against the man	appealing to prejudice or emotion
ad rem	to the matter	relevant or pertinent

THE LANGUAGE OF CHRISTIANITY

Because Greek was the primary language of many of the earliest Christian writers, much of the terminology of Christianity is Greek in origin.

Vocabulary

Greek or Latin word	English meaning
credo-credere-creditum	believe, trust
Christos (Χριστός)	anointed
biblos (βίβλος)	book
dogma (δόγμα)	decree, opinion
cf. doceo-docēre-doctum = show, teach	
apostello (ἀποστέλλω)	send out
martys, martyros (μάρτυς)	witness
oecumene (οἰκουμένη)	inhabited world
Which Greek noun can you see in this word?	
angelos (ἄγγελος)	messenger
ecclesia (ἐκκλησία)	assembly
episcopos (ἐπίσκοπος)	guardian, overseer; bishop
Which Greek verb can you see in this word?	
dioecesis (διοίκησις)	government, organization, province
hieros (ἱερός)	sacred, holy
hagios (ἅγιος)	sacred, holy; saint
sacer, sacri	sacred, holy
templum, templi	temple
basilica, basilicae	large oblong public building in the Roman Forum used for judicial proceedings
cf. basileus (βασιλεύς) = king	
cyrios (κύριος)	master, lord
cyriacon (κυριακόν)	belonging to the lord > > > Old English *cirice*

Note

The root of the word *church* is almost unrecognizable in its Anglicized form; the Greek-based word was introduced into Old English at the time of the conversion of the Anglo-Saxons to Christianity in 597 A.D.

EXERCISES

A. 1. The plutocrats looked down from the Olympian heights of their corporate board room as they watched the plebeians on the stock-exchange floor panic at the mercurial behavior of the prices of cereal futures. Despite their saturnine expressions, the titans of industry actually felt quite jovial at this turn of events.

Which divinities or mythical places appear in this paragraph and what does each of them represent?

Divinity   *Meaning of word*

_____ _____

_____ _____

_____ _____

_____ _____

_____ _____

_____ _____

_____ _____

B. In Exercises 2–50 answer each question or fill in the blank(s).

2. What do Janus and a janitor have in common? _____

_____

3. Why did the strongman Charles Atlas choose that particular name? _____

_____

4. When sitting in the dentist's chair, what kind of philosophical attitude is it best to adopt? _____

5. An _____ enjoys the finer things in life.

6. What is the chief symptom of lethargy? _____

7. A vulnerable spot, either physical or emotional, is called an _____

   _____.

8. What quality should a woman named *Sophia* possess? _____

9. _____ gave his name to a word meaning a long, wandering journey.

10. To speak in *stentorian* tones is to talk _____.

11. A battle that is won at great cost is called a _____.

12. A man of few words may be said to be _____.

13. Cutting off a thief's hand for stealing a loaf of bread may be termed a _____

    punishment.

14. The subway stations in New York are often so dirty that they may be compared to the

    _____.

15. A committee that is formed to deal with one particular issue is called _____

    _____.

16. An argument that focuses on the personal qualities of the opposition is called an

    _____ attack.

17. *Angels* are the _____ of God.

18. A *museum* is a _____ for the _____.

19. *I should of went* is an example of a _____.

20. According to its root meaning, *morals* are merely a matter of _____.

21. A prophet of doom and gloom may be called a _____.

22. Someone who gives wise advice and counsel may be called a _____.

23. A *martial* spirit is a useful attribute in _____.

24. When Julius Caesar was warned, "Beware the Ides of March," on what day should he

    have stayed home? _____

25. A *credulous* individual is _____ _____.

26. When the Catholic Church grants a "*nihil* obstat" to a book, it means that _____

    _____ stands in the way of publishing it.

27. *Ephemeral* ideas last _____ _____.

28. A *hedonist* lives only for _____ .

29. When discussion of an issue will not affect its outcome, we may call it an _____ _____ argument.

30. After Richard Nixon was defeated in a gubernatorial election, he announced he would never again run for office; but not many years later, like the _____, he rose from the ashes of his political career.

31. Some public figures have a _____ ability to change position on almost any issue.

32. A faithful, loving woman who patiently awaits her husband may be described as resembling _____ .

33. A greedy, grasping individual may be described as a _____ .

34. To *hector* someone is to attempt to _____ him.

35. A speech of violent denunciation may be called a _____ .

36. What does the expression, "to open up a Pandora's box," mean? _____ _____

37. Your *horoscope* is determined by _____ _____ of your birth.

38. If you put off *for tomorrow* what you should do today, you are a _____ .

39. What is the current English meaning of *secular*? _____

40. The term *medieval* was coined to indicate that _____ in the _____ between antiquity and the modern world.

41. Con*templ*ation should take place in a _____. What is the current English meaning of this word? _____

42. The account of his life read like a *hagio*graphy since it concealed all his faults and portrayed him as a _____ .

43. "It's been *aeons* since I saw you," she cried. She was exaggerating, but it really had been _____ .

44. The *Apostles* were _____ _____ to preach the Gospel.

45. A *dogmatic* individual wants to impose his own _____ on others.

46. What do the abbreviations a.m. and p.m. represent? _____ and _____

47. I undertook the *Sisyphean* task of cleaning up my room even though I knew it was _____

48. It was clear from their *sybaritic* life style that they enjoyed _____ .

49. It was truly an *ecumenical* meeting, since delegates came from the entire _____

_____ .

50. He indulged his _____ tastes by ordering the best food and wine on the menu.

Portrait bust of Tiberius, Roman Emperor (A.D. 14–37).

Moth: They have been at a great feast of languages and stolen the scraps.

Costard: O, they have lived long on the almsbasket of words! I marvel thy master hath not eaten thee for a word; for thou art not so long by the head as honorificabilitudinitatibus; thou art easier swallowed than a flapdragon.

WILLIAM SHAKESPEARE,
Love's Labour's Lost V.i

LATIN PHRASES USED IN ENGLISH

LATIN PROVERBS

deo volente = God willing!
cum grano salis = with a grain of salt
de gustibus non est disputandum = About tastes, it ought not to be argued.
errare humanum est = To err is human.
nihil sub sole novum = There is nothing new under the sun.
vita brevis, ars longa = Life is short; art, long.
de mortuis nil nisi bonum = about the dead, nothing but good
nos morituri te salutamus = We who are about to die salute you.

MEASUREMENTS OF TIME

ab ovo = from the egg (from the beginning)
in principio = in the beginning
ante bellum = before the war
post bellum = after the war
anno domini = in the year of (our) Lord
status quo = state in which
pro tempore = for the time (being)
terminus ante quem = end before which

terminus post quem = end after which
ad infinitum = to infinity
per diem = by the day
carpe diem = Seize the day. (Enjoy the moment.)
tempus fugit = Time flies.
finis = the end

MEASURES AND RELATIONSHIPS

in toto = in the whole (completely)
per se = by itself (intrinsically)
quid pro quo = something for something (one thing in return for another)
ne plus ultra = not more beyond (the highest point)
ex parte = out of the part (on one side only)
passim = here and there
per capita = by heads
ex post facto = from a thing done afterwards (subsequently)
ad nauseam = to the point of disgust

SPEECH AND LANGUAGE

ipse dixit = he himself said
lapsus linguae = slip of the tongue
lingua franca = the Frankish tongue (the commonly spoken language)
mirabile dictu = wonderful to tell
non sequitur = it does not follow (illogical conclusion)
verbatim = word for word
viva voce = with living voice (orally)
vox populi = the voice of the people

DRAMA AND THEATER

dramatis personae = the masks (characters) of the drama
deus ex machina = the god out of the machine (an improbable solution)
exit = He/she goes out.

exeunt = They go out.
exeunt omnes = They all go out.
in medias res = in the middle of things

PEOPLE, PLACES, AND THINGS

alumnus = foster son
alumna = foster daughter
alma mater = nourishing mother
persona non grata = a person not pleasing (a person not welcome)
alter ego = another I
rara avis = rare bird (a unique individual)
sui generis = of its own kind (unique)
quid nunc = What now? (a gossip)
inter alios = among other people
inter alia = among other things
in situ = in place
sub rosa = under the rose (confidentially; secretly)
terra firma = solid land
terra incognita = unknown land
in absentia = in the absence of
tabula rasa = blank slate
vade mecum = Come with me. (manual, handbook)
magnum opus = great work
summum bonum = highest good
desideratum = that which was desired
mea culpa = my fault
modus operandi = way of operating
modus vivendi = way of living
sine qua non = without which not (something essential)
noli me tangere = Don't touch me.

LATIN ABBREVIATIONS AND WORDS USED IN SCHOLARLY RESEARCH AND WRITING

A.D. (anno domini) = in the year of (our) Lord
c. or ca. (circa) = around

cf. (confer) = compare

ed. cit. (editio citata) = the edition cited

e.g. (exempli gratia) = for the sake of an example

et al. (et alii or et alia) = and others (people or things)

etc. (et cetera) = and the rest

et seq. (et sequens or et sequentia) = and following (singular or plural)

fl. (floruit) = he (she) flourished

ibid. (ibidem) = in the same place

i.e. (id est) = that is

inf. (infra) = below

loc. cit. (loco citato) = in the place cited

n.b. or N.B. (nota bene) = note well

op. cit. (opere citato) = in the work cited

q.e.d. (quod erat demonstrandum) = that which was to be proved or shown

q.v. (quod vide) = which see

sic = thus

sc. (scilicet) = namely (scire licet = it is permitted to know)

sup. (supra) = above

seriatim = in a series

viz. (videlicet) = namely (videre licet = it is permitted to see)

LATIN VOCABULARY

A

a = not
a, ab = away, away from
abdomen, abdominis = belly
abhorreo-abhorrēre = shrink back from
acer, acris = sharp, bitter
ad = to, toward
adolesco, adolescere, adultum = grow up
aedificium, aedificii = building
aequus, aequi = equal
aer, aeris = air
aestas, aestatis = summer
aevum, aevi = period of time
ager, agri = field
  agro- (learned borrowing) = soil, crop
ago-agere-actum = do, drive
albus, albi = white
alias = at another time
alibi = elsewhere
alo-alere-altum = nourish
ambitio, ambitionis = going around
ambo = both
amicus, amici = friend
amo-amare-amatum = love
amor-amoris = love

anima, animae = breath
animal, animalis = animal
animus, animi = soul, spirit
annus, anni = year
ante = before
apis, apis = bee
aqua, aquae = water
arbitror-arbitrari-arbitratum = think
arbor, arboris = tree
architectura, architecturae = the art
  of building
ardeo-ardēre = burn
arena, arenae = sand; arena
argentum, argenti = silver
ars, artis = art, skill
atrium, atrii = entrance hall
audax, audacis = bold
audeo-audēre = dare
audio-audire-auditum = hear
augeo-augēre-auctum = increase; enrich
augur, auguris = prophet
auris, auris = ear
aurus, auri = gold
autumnus, autumni = autumn
auxilium, auxilii = help, aid; troops

avarus, avari = greedy
aveo-avēre = be well
avis, avis = bird

B

bacillus, bacilli = little staff
baculum, baculi = staff, walking stick
bellum, belli = war
bene = well
bilis, bilis = bile
bis = twice
bonus, boni = good
brevis, brevis = short

C

cado-cadere-casum = fall
caecum, caeci = blind; concealed
caedo-caedere-caesum = cut; kill
caeruleus, caerulei = blue
calculus, calculi = stone, pebble
calor, caloris = heat
calx, calcis = stone, pebble
camera, camerae = vault; private room
campus, campi = plain, field
candeo-candēre = glow, shine
candesco-candescere = to begin to glow
  or shine
canis, canis = dog
canto-cantare-cantatum = sing
capio-capere-captum = seize, take
caput, capitis = head
caro, carnis = meat
castus, casti = pure
cedo-cedere-cessum = yield; go
cella, cellae = small room
censor, censoris = censor
centum = hundred
cerebrum, cerebri = brain
charta, chartae = map
circa = around (approximately)
circum = around (distance)
circus, circi = circle

civis, civis = citizen
civitas, civitatis = city, state
clamo-clamare-clamatum = call out,
  shout
clarus, clari = clear, bright
claudo, claudere, clausum = close
clavus, clavi = key; collarbone
clemens, clementis = mild, gentle
coalesco, coalescere, coalitum = grow
  together, become one
codex, codicis = book
cohors, cohortis = group, company
collegium, collegii = corporation, group
colo-colere-cultum = inhabit, dwell
colonia, coloniae = estate; settlement
color, coloris = color
communis, communis = shared, common, public
computo-computare-computatum = sum
  up, calculate
congredior-congredi-congressum = meet
consul, consulis = consul
contagio, contagionis = touching, contact
contra = against
copia, copiae = abundance
cornu, cornūs = horn
corona, coronae = crown
corpus, corporis = body
cors, cordis = heart
cras = tomorrow
credo-credere-creditum = believe
creo-creare-creatum = bring forth, make
cresco-crescere-cretum = arise, become
  visible
crimen, criminis = accusation
cubo-cubare-cubitum = lie down
culpa, culpae = fault, blame
cum = with
cumulus, cumuli = pile
cupido, cupidinis = desire
cura, curae = care
curriculum, curriculi = running, race
curro-currere-cursum = run
custos, custodis = guard
cutis, cutis = skin

D

de = about, concerning; down from
debeo-debēre-debitum = owe
decem = ten
decimus = tenth
decus, decoris = ornament, splendor, honor
deformis, deformis = deformed
deleo-delēre-deletum = destroy
delinquo, delinquere, delictum = fail, commit a crime
dens, dentis = tooth
despicio-despicere-despectum = look down on, despise
deus, dei = god
dico-dicere-dictum = say, speak
dictator, dictatoris = dictator
dies, diei = day
digero-digerere-digestum = separate, divide
digitus, digiti = finger, toe
dignitas, dignitatis = worth, merit
dis = apart, away
disciplina, disciplinae = instruction, learning
discipulus, discipula = pupil
disco-discere = learn
divido-dividere-divisum = separate, allot
divortium, divortii = divorce
divus, divi = divine (adjective), god (noun)
do-dare-datum = give
doceo-docēre-doctum = show, teach
doctrina, doctrinae = teaching, instruction
dominor-dominari-dominatum = rule
dominus, domini = head of the household; master
domus, domūs = home
dormio-dormire-dormitum = sleep
duco-ducere-ductum = lead
duo = two
duodeni = twelve

E

edo-edere-editum = bring forth; publish
edo-edere-esum = eat

educo-educare-educatum = train, rear; educate
effervesco, effervescere = boil up, foam
ego, mei = I
eques, equitis = horseman
equus, equi = horse
erro, errare, erratum = stray, wander
erudio-erudire-eruditum = polish; educate
ex, e = out of, from
examino-examinare-examinatum =weigh, consider
experior-experiri-expertum = try
extra = outside

F

fabula, fabulae = story
facio-facere-factum = make, do
facultas, facultatis = skill, ability
fallo-fallere-falsum = deceive
fama, famae = rumor, report
familia, familiae = family
fateor-fatēri-fassum = admit, say, speak
felis, felis = cat
felix, felicis = happy
femina, feminae = woman
fenestra, fenestrae = window
fermentum, fermenti = leaven, yeast
fero-ferre-latum = carry, bear
ferrum, ferri = iron
ferveo-fervēre = boil; rage
fibula, fibulae = clamp
fidelis, fidelis = faithful
fides, fidei = faith
fiducia, fiduciae = trust, confidence; security
filia, filiae = daughter
filius, filii = son
finio-finire-finitum = limit, fix; close
fiscus, fisci = basket, purse; treasury
flecto-flectere-flexum = change, alter
flo-flare-flatum = blow
floreo-florēre = bloom
flos, floris = flower
fodio-fodere-fossum = dig
folium, folii = leaf

for-fari-fatum = speak
forma, formae = shape, beauty
fortis, fortis = brave
fortuna, fortunae = chance, luck; fate
forum, fori = outside space; market
   place; place of assembly
fossa, fossae = ditch
frango-frangere-fractum = break
frater, fratris = brother
fraus, fraudis = deceit
fundo-fundare-fundatum = lay the bottom; fix, establish
fundus, fundi = bottom, the deep
fungor-fungi-functum = perform, do
fungus, fungi = sponge

G

gens, gentis = clan, tribe, nation
genu, genūs = knee
genus, generis = type, kind
gero-gerere-gestum = bear, carry, wage
glacies, glaciei = ice
gladius, gladii = sword
gnosco-gnoscere-gnotum = get to know
gradior-gradi-gressum = walk, step
gratus, grati = pleasing
gravis, gravis = heavy
grex, gregis = flock
gubernator, gubernatoris = pilot

H

haereo-haerēre-haesum = cling to, stick
heres, heredis = heir; possessor; successor
hibernus, hiberni = wintry
homo, hominis = man
hora, horae = hour
horreo-horrēre = shudder
hortor-hortari-hortatum = urge
hospes, hospitis = guest
hostis, hostis = enemy
hybrida, hybridae = mixed breed

I

id = it
idem = the same

ignis, ignis = fire
ileum, ilei = flank
imago, imaginis = copy, likeness
imbecilis, imbecilis = weak
imperator, imperatoris = leader,
   commander
imperium, imperii = command
impero-imperare-imperatum = command
in = in, on
in- = not
individuus, individui = not separable
inertia, inertiae = lack of skill; laziness
infamia, infamiae = shame, disgrace
ingenium, ingenii = nature
inimicus, inimici = unfriendly
insectus, insecti = notched, cut
intellego-intellegere-intellectum
   = distinguish, understand
inter = between
intestinum, intestini = internal
intra = among, within
iter, itineris = route; way; journey

J

jacio-jacere-jactum = throw, hurl
jejunum, jejuni = hungry, dry; barren
judex, judicis = judge
jugulum, juguli = throat
jungo-jungere-junctum = join, unite
jus, juris = law
juvenis, juvenis = young

L

labor, laborari, laboratum = work (v.)
labor, laboris = work (n.)
labor-labi-lapsum = fall down, slip
lac, lactis = milk
lapis, lapidis = stone
lascivus, lascivi = wicked
legio, legionis = body of soldiers
lego-legere-lectum = choose; read
lenis, lenis = gentle
levis, levis = light
levo-levare-levatum = raise, lighten
lex, legis = law

liber, liberi = free
liber, libri = book
libero-liberare-liberatum = set free
libertas, libertatis = freedom
libido, libidinis = desire
ligo-ligare-ligatum = bind
limen, liminis = threshold
lingua, linguae = tongue
liquidus, liquidi = fluid, flowing
liquor-liqui = flow, melt
littera, litterae = letter
loquor-loqui-locutum = speak
lucrum, lucri = profit, advantage
ludo-ludere-lusum = play; make believe,
  mock
ludus, ludi = sport, game; school
lumen, luminis = light
luna, lunae = moon
lux, lucis = light
luxuria, luxuriae = extravagance, excess
lympha, lymphae = fluid; water

M

magister, magistri = teacher (male)
magistra, magistrae = teacher (female)
magnus, magni = large
major, majoris = larger, bigger
malus, mali = bad, evil
mando-mandare-mandatum = order,
  charge
manus, manūs = hand
mare, maris = sea
margo, marginis = border, edge
maritus, mariti = husband
mater, matris = mother
materia, materiae = matter
matrimonium, matrimonii = marriage
matrona, matronae = married woman
maximus, maximi = greatest, largest
medicus, medici = doctor
medium, medii = middle; in the open;
  public
melior, melioris = better
memoria, memoriae = memory
mendax, mendacis = lying

mens, mentis = mind
mensis, mensis = month
merces, mercedis = pay, wages
mereor-mererī-meritum = earn, deserve
mergo-mergere-mersum = sink, over-
  whelm; cover
miles, militis = soldier
mille = thousand
minimum, minimi = least
minor = fewer
minus = less
miror-mirari-miratum = wonder at
mitto-mittere-missum = send
modus, modi = measure, boundary;
  manner, way
moles, molis = mass, area
moneo-monēre-monitum = warn
monumentum, monumenti = monument
mordeo-mordēre-morsum = bite
morior-mori-mortuum = die
mors, mortis = death
mos, moris = custom
moveo-movēre-motum = move
multus, multi = much, many
mundus, mundi = world
municipium, municipii = town
munus, muneris = reward, gift
murus, muri = wall
musculus, musculi = muscle; mouse
muto-mutare-mutatum = change

N

nascor-nasci-natum = be born
nasus, nasi = nose
natura, naturae = nature
nauta, nautae = sailor
nebula, nebulae = mist
negotium, negotii = business
nervus, nervi = nerve
neuter, neutri = neither
niger, nigri = black
nihil = nothing
nimbus, nimbi = halo, cloud
nix, nivis = snow
nomen, nominis = name

nomino-nominare-nominatum = name, speak about

non = not

nonus, noni = ninth

novem = nine

novus, novi = new

nox, noctis = night

nucleus, nuclei = kernel

nullus, nullius = none

numerus, numeri = number

nuntio, nuntiare, nuntiatum = announce, speak

nuptiae, nuptiarum = wedding

nutrio-nutrire = nourish

nux, nucis = nut

O

ob = to, toward; against

obsolesco, obsolescere, obsoletum = wear out

octavus, octavi = eighth

octo = eight

oculus, oculi = eye

odium, odii = hatred

omnis, omnis = all

oppono-opponere-oppositum = oppose

ops, opis = property, wealth

optimus, optimi = best

opto-optare-optatum = choose; wish for

opus, operis = work

ordo, ordinis = rank, order

origo, originis = source, beginning

orior-oriri-ortum = rise, come forth

oro-orare-oratum = speak

os, oris = mouth

os, ossis = bone

otium, otii = leisure

P

pagus, pagi = country district

pars, partis = part

parvus, parvi = small

patella, patellae = small pan; kneecap

pater, patris = father

patior-pati-passum = suffer, undergo; permit

patricius, patricii = patrician, noble

pax, pacis = peace

pecco, peccare, peccatum = make a mistake

peculium, peculii = private property

pecunia, pecuniae = money

pecus, pecoris = flock, herd

pejor, pejoris = worse

pello-pellere-pulsum = strike, push

pendo-pendere-pensum = hang down, weigh

per = through; intensive

percutio-percutere-percussum = strike

periculum, periculi = danger

persona, personae = mask

pes, pedis = foot

pessimus, pessimi = worst

peto-petere-petitum = seek, strive

pigmentum, pigmenti = color, paint

pingo-pingere-pictum = represent, paint

pinna, pinnae = feather; wings

piscis, piscis = fish

plaudo-plaudere-plausum = clap, strike

plebs, plebis = common people

plico-plicare-plicatum = fold

plumbum, plumbi = lead

plurimus, plurimi = most

plus, pluris = more

pluvia, pluviae = rain

poeta, poetae = poet

pono-ponere-positum = put, place

pontifex, pontificis = pontiff

populus, populi = people

porta, portae = door

porto-portare-portatum = carry

post = after

postulo-postulare-postulatum = demand; ask, inquire

potens, potentis = powerful

potio, potionis = drink

prae = before

premo-premere-pressum = press, hide

pretium, pretii = money; worth, value
primus, primi = first
princeps, principis = chief
pro = before, in front of, on behalf of
proficio-proficere-profectum = make headway, advance
profiteor-profitēri-professum = declare openly, announce
proles, prolis = offspring
proprietas, proprietatis = characteristic, possession
proprius, proprii = one's own
prosper, prosperi = fortunate, favorable
prurio-prurire-pruritum = itch
pudeo-pudēre-puditum = feel shame
puer, pueri = boy
pugno-pugnare-pugnatum = fight
pulcher, pulchri = beautiful
pulmo, pulmonis = lung
pupa, pupae = girl
pupus, pupi = boy
puto-putare-putatum = consider, think

Q

quaero-quaerere-quaesitum = seek, ask
qualis, qualis = of what kind?
quantum, quanti = how much?
quartus, quarti = fourth
quasi = as if; resembling
quattuor = four
quies, quietis = rest, quiet, peace
quiesco-quiescere-quietum = rest, be at peace
quinque = five
quintus, quinti = fifth
quot = how many?

R

radix, radicis = root
rapio-rapere-raptum = seize, snatch
rarus, rari = rare
ratio, rationis = account, plan, understanding
recipio-recipere-receptum = take back, regain
rectus, recti = straight
rego-regere-rectum = rule
religio, religionis = religion
relinquo-relinquere-relictum = leave
remedium, remedii = cure
renum, reni = kidney
reptilis, reptilis = snake
repudium, repudii = divorce
res publica = republic
retro = back, backward
revertor-reverti-reversum = return, come back
rex, regis = king
rigeo-rigēre = grow stiff, stiffen
ruber, rubri = red
rudis, rudis = rough; unskilled
rumpo-rumpere-ruptum = break
rus, ruris = countryside

S

saccus, sacci = bag, sack
sacer, sacri = sacred, holy
saeculum, saeculi = generation; spirit of an age
sal, salis = salt
salax, salacis = lustful
salus, salutis = health, safety
sanguis, sanguinis = blood
sanus, sani = healthy
scio-scire-scitum = know
scribo-scribere-scriptum = write
sculpo-sculpere-sculptum = form, fashion
seco-secare-sectum = cut
secundus, secundi = second
sedeo-sedēre-sessum = sit
semen, seminis = seed
semi = half
senatus, senatūs = senate
seneo-senēre = be old
senesco-senescere = grow old
senex, senis = old
sentio-sentire-sensum = feel
septem = seven

septimus, septimi = seventh
sequor-sequi-secutum = follow
serpo-serpere-serptum = creep
servio-servire-servitum = be a slave, serve
servo-servare-servatum = watch; protect;
  keep
servus, servi = slave
sesqui = one and a half
sex = six
sextus, sexti = sixth
signum, signi = sign, seal, mark
simia, simiae = monkey
sine = without
situs, situs = position, place
socius, socii = ally, companion
sol, solis = sun
solidus, solidi = firm; whole, complete
solus, solius = alone, only
solvo-solvere-solutum = loosen, untie,
  release
somnus, somni = sleep
sono-sonare-sonitum = sound
sopor, soporis = deep sleep
soror, sororis = sister
species, speciei = form, appearance
specio-specere-spectum = look at
specto-spectare-spectatum = look at
speculor-speculari-speculatum = watch,
  observe
spero-sperare-speratum = hope
spiro-spirare-spiratum = breathe
spondeo-spondere-sponsum = pledge
stella, stellae = star
sto-stare-statum = stand
stomachus, stomachi = opening, belly
stringo-stringere-strictum = draw tight,
  bind; cut off
struo-struere-structum = build; arrange
studeo-studere = be eager for, be diligent
stupeo-stupere = be stunned
suadeo-suadere-suasum = advise, urge
sub = under
sum-esse-futurum = be, exist
sumo-sumere-sumptum = take, use
super = above (preposition)

superior, superioris = higher
superus, superi = above (adjective)
supremus, supremi = highest

T

tango-tangere-tactum = touch
taxo-taxare-taxatum = tax
tego-tegere-tectum = cover
templum, templi = temple
tempus, temporis = time
teneo-tenere-tentum = hold
ter = thrice
tergum, tergi = back
termino-terminare-terminatum = limit;
  fix, set
terra, terrae = land
terreo-terrere-territum = frighten
tertius, tertii = third
testor-testari-testatum = show, prove;
  witness
texo-texere-textum = weave
tibia, tibiae = shinbone; flute
tolero-tolerare-toleratum = bear
traho-trahere-tractum = draw, drag
trans = across
tres = three
tribunus, tribuni = tribune
tribuo-tribuere-tributum = give, pay
tueor-tueri-tuitum = look after, guard
turba, turbae = crowd
turpis, turpis = wicked
tutor, tutoris = guardian, protector

U

ulterior, ulterioris = farther
ultimus, ultimi = farthest
ultra = beyond
universitas, universitatis = the whole;
  community
unus, unius = one
urbs, urbis = city
ursa, ursae = bear
usura, usurae = interest paid for the use
  of money
utor-uti-usum = use, employ

uxor, uxoris = wife

V

vacca, vaccae = cow
vaco-vacare-vacatum = be empty
valeo-valēre = be strong
vapor, vaporis = gas
varius, varii = different
vas, vasis = vessel
veho-vehere-vectum = carry
velox, velocis = swift, rapid
vena, venae = vein
venio-venire-ventum = come
ventus, venti = wind
ver, veris = spring
verbum, verbi = word
verso-versare-versatum = turn
verto-vertere-versum = turn
verus, veri = true
vestigium, vestigii = trace, track
vestio-vestire-vestitum = dress, cover

vestis, vestis = clothes, garment, covering
vetus, veteris = old
via, viae = street; road
vicinia, viciniae = neighborhood
video-vidēre-visum = see
villa, villae = farmhouse
vinco-vincere-victum = conquer
vir, viri = man
viridis, viridis = green
virilis, virilis = manly
virtus, virtutis = manliness; excellence, worth
virus, viri = poison
vita, vitae = life
vivo-vivere-victum = live
voco-vocare-vocatum = call
volvo-volvere-volutum = turn
voro-vorare-voratum = devour
votum, voti = promise
vox, vocis = voice
vulgus, vulgi = people, public
vulnus, vulneris = wound

GREEK VOCABULARY

The vocabulary is arranged in English alphabetical order. If the stem of a noun is used to form learned borrowings in English, the genitive case is given.

A (α)

a- (ἀ-) or an- before vowels = not
acros (ἄκρος) = end, top
adelphe (ἀδελφή) = sister
adelphos (ἀδελφός) = brother
aden (ἀδήν) = gland
aegis (αἰγίς) = shield
aeon (αἰών) = an age; a long period of time
aer (ἀήρ) = air
aesthesis (αἴσθησις) = feeling
aetia (αἰτία) = cause, origin
ago (ἄγω) = do, drive; lead
agora (ἀγορά) = marketplace; place of assembly
agov (ἀγών) = assembly; contest
ailuros (αἴλουρος) = cat
algos (ἄλγος) = pain
amphi (ἀμφί) = around; on both sides
amphoreus (ἀμφορεύς) = two-handled storage jar
ana (ἀνά) = up; back; again

anemos (ἄνεμος) = wind
aner, andros (ἀνήρ) = man
angelos (ἄγγελος) = messenger
anthos (ἄνθος) = blossom
anthropos (ἄνθρωπος) = man
anti (ἀντί) = against
apo (ἀπό) = from, away from
apologeomai (ἀπολογέομαι) = defend
apologia (ἀπολογία) = defense
apostello (ἀποστέλλω) = send out
arachne (ἀράχνη) = spider
arche (ἀρχή) = rule; beginning
archeos (ἀρχαῖος) = old
archon (ἄρχων) = ruler, chief
arctos (ἄρκτος) = bear
argyros (ἄργυρος) = silver
aristos (ἄριστος) = best
arithmos (ἀριθμός) = number
arteria (ἀρτηρία) = windpipe
aster (ἀστήρ) = star
astron (ἄστρον) = star
athlos (ἄθλος) = contest

atmos (ἀτμός) = vapor
atomos (ἄτομος) = uncut
auto (αὐτό) = self

B (β)
bacterion (βακτήριον) = rod
baino (βαίνω) = go
baros (βάρος) = weight
basileus (βασιλεύς) = king
biblion (βιβλίον) = book
biblos (βίβλος) = book
bios (βίος) = life
blastos (βλαστός) = sprout; seed
botane (βοτάνη) = grass, herb
bous (βοῦς) = cow
brachys (βραχύς) = short
bradys (βραδύς) = slow
bronchoi (βρόγχοι) = duct

C (x) and CH (χ)
cacos (κακός) = bad
canon (κανών) = rule; standard
cardia (καρδία) = heart
cata (κατά) or cath- (καθ-) = down,
  away, against; concerning
catharsis (κάθαρσις) = cleansing; purification
cephale (κεφαλή) = head
ceramia (κεραμεία) = pottery
chalcos (χαλκός) = copper
chaos (χάος) = chaos
character (χαρακτήρ) = mark
charisma (χάρισμα) = grace
chartes (χάρτης) = papyrus roll
chemia (χημεία) = alloying
chilioi (χίλιοι) = thousand
chir (χείρ) = hand
chloros (χλωρός) = green
cholae (χολαί) = gall bladder
chole (χολή) = bile
choreuo (χορεύω) = dance in a circle
christos (χριστός) = anointed
chroma (χρῶμα) = color
chronos (χρόνος) = time
chrysos (χρυσός) = gold

cithara (κιθάρα) = lyre, lute
clima (κλίμα) = zone, region
cline (κλίνη) = couch, bed
colon (κόλον) = colon
coma (κῶμα) = deep sleep
comoedia (κωμῳδία) = comedy
comos (κῶμος) = revel; merrymaking
cosmos (κόσμος) = order
crater (κρατήρ) = mixing bowl
cratos (κράτος) = strength, rule
crino (κρίνω) = judge
crisis (κρίσις) = decision; trial; dispute
cryptos (κρυπτός) = hidden
cyanos (κύανος) = blue
cybernetes (κυβερνήτης) = pilot
cyclos (κύκλος) = circle
cymbalon (κύμβαλον) = cymbal
cyon, cynos (κύων) = dog
cystis (κύστις) = bladder
cytos (κύτος) = hollow

D (δ)
daemon (δαίμων) = spirit
daphne (δάφνη) = laurel
deca (δέκα) = ten
decatos (δέκατος) = tenth
demos (δῆμος) = people
dendron (δένδρον) = tree
derma, dermatos (δέρμα) = skin
despotes (δεσπότης) = master, lord
deuteros (δεύτερος) = second
dia (διά) = through; intensive
diaphragma (διάφραγμα) = diaphragm
didactos (διδακτός) = taught
dinos (δεινός) = terrible
dioecesis (διοίκησις) = management,
  government
dis (δίς) = twice
discos (δίσκος) = plate
dogma (δόγμα) = decree; teaching
dracon (δράκων) = dragon
drama (δρᾶμα) = deed, act
dromos (δρόμος) = running
drys, dryos (δρῦς) = oak tree
dynamis (δύναμις) = strength, force

dyo (δύο) = two
dys- (δυσ-) = hard, difficult

E (ε, η, or οι)

ec (ἐκ) or ex (ἐξ) = out of, from
ecclesia (ἐκκλησία) = assembly
ecos (οἶκος) = house
electron (ἤλεκτρον) = amber
empiros (ἔμπειρος) = experienced
emporion (ἐμπόριον) = market
en (ἐν) = in
enatos (ἔνατος) = ninth
encephalos (ἐγκέφαλος) = brain
encomion (ἐγκώμιον) = a speech of
    praise
encyclios (ἐγκύκλιος) = encircling
ennea (ἐννέα) = nine
enteron (ἔντερον) = intestine
entomos (ἔντομος) = cut up
epi (ἐπί) = on; upon; for; in addition to
episcopos (ἐπίσκοπος) = overseer,
    watcher, guardian
episteme (ἐπιστήμη) = knowledge; science
ergon (ἔργον) = work
eros (ἔρως) = love
erythros (ἐρυθρός) = red
ethnos (ἔθνος) = race, nation
ethos (ἦθος) = custom; behavior
eu (εὖ) = well

G (γ)

gala, galactos (γάλα) = milk
gamete (γαμετή) = wife
gametes (γαμετής) = husband
gamos (γάμος) = marriage
gaster, gastros (γαστήρ) = belly
ge (γῆ) = earth
genea (γενεά) = family
genos (γένος) = race; kind
geron (γέρων) = old man
geusis (γεῦσις) = sense of taste
glossa (γλῶσσα) = tongue
glycys (γλυκύς) = sweet
gnosis (γνῶσις) = knowledge
gonia (γωνία) = angle

gonu (γόνυ) = knee
gramma (γράμμα) = letter
grapho (γράφω) = write
gymnazo (γυμνάζω) = exercise
gyne, gynecos (γυνή) = woman

H (ʽ)

hagios (ἅγιος) = sacred, holy; saint
harmonia (ἁρμονία) = joining, fitting
    together; harmony
hebdomos (ἕβδομος) = seventh
hecaton (ἑκατόν) = hundred
hedone (ἡδονή) = pleasure
helios (ἥλιος) = sun
helix (ἕλιξ) = spiral
hema, hematos (αἷμα) = blood
hemera (ἡμέρα) = day
hemi (ἡμι-) = half
hen (ἕν) = one
hepar, hepatos (ἧπαρ) = liver
hepta (ἑπτά) = seven
heresis (αἵρεσις) = choice
herpo (ἕρπω) = creep, crawl
heteros (ἕτερος) = other
hex (ἕξ) = six
hieros (ἱερός) = sacred, holy
hippos (ἵππος) = horse
histemi (ἵστημι) = to make stand
historia (ἱστορία) = inquiry
histos (ἱστός) = web
hodos (ὁδός) = way, path, route
homeos (ὅμοιος) = similar
homos (ὁμός) = same
hybris (ὕβρις) = shamelessness; exag-
    gerated pride
hydor, hydatos (ὕδωρ) = water
hygieia (ὑγίεια) = health
hygros (ὑγρός) = liquid
hyle (ὕλη) = matter
hymnos (ὕμνος) = a song in praise of a
    deity
hyper (ὑπέρ) = above; excessively
hypnos (ὕπνος) = sleep
hypo (ὑπό) = below; deficient
hypocrites (ὑποκριτής) = actor

hypokrinomai (ὑποκρίνομαι) = reply, answer

hystera (ὑστέρα) = uterus

I (ι)

iatros (ἰατρός) = physician

ichthys (ἰχθύς) = fish

idea (ἰδέα) = form, class, kind

idios (ἴδιος) = private, personal

idiotes (ἰδιώτης) = private citizen

isos (ἴσος) = equal

K (κ)

kineo (κινέω) = move

kinesis (κίνησις) = movement

L (λ)

leptos (λεπτός) = slender

leucos (λευκός) = white

lithos (λίθος) = stone

logos (λόγος) = word; reason

lyo (λύω) = untie

lysis (λύσις) = untying; loosening

M (μ)

macron (μακρόν) = long, large

malacos (μαλακός) = soft

mania (μανία) = madness

manthano (μανθάνω) = learn

martys (μάρτυς) = witness

mater (μάτηρ) = mother

mathesis (μάθησις) = learning

mechane (μεχανή) = device

megalos (μεγάλος) = huge

megas (μέγας) = huge, big

melancholos (μελάγχολος) = of black bile

melas, melanos (μέλας) = black

melodia (μελωδία) = song

meta (μετά) or meth- (μεθ᾽) = with, after, beyond; change

meteoron (μετέωρον) = raised in the air

metron (μέτρον) = measure

micron (μικρόν) = small

mimesis (μίμησις) = representation; imitation

miseo (μισέω) = hate

Mnemosyne (Μνημοσύνη) = Memory

molybdos (μόλυβδος) = lead

monos (μόνος) = only, single

moros (μωρός) = fool

morphe (μορφή) = shape, form

Mousa (Μοῦσα) = Muse

musice (μουσική) = the art of the Muses

myelos (μυελός) = marrow

mys, myos (μῦς) = mouse

mythos (μῦθος) = story

N (ν)

neos (νέος) = new

nephros (νεφρός) = kidney

neuron (νεῦρον) = nerve

nomikos (νομικός) = of the law

nomos (νόμος) = rule, statute

O (ο)

octo (ὀκτώ) = eight

odous, odontos (ὀδούς) = tooth

odyne (ὀδύνη) = pain

oecumene (οἰκουμένη) = the civilized world

ogdoos (ὄγδοος) = eighth

oligoi (ὀλίγοι) = few

onyma (ὄνυμα) = name

ophthalmos (ὀφθαλμός) = eye

opsis (ὄψις) = sight

opteuo (ὀπτεύω) = see

orchestra (ὀρχήστρα) = place where the chorus danced

orexis (ὄρεξις) = appetite

organon (ὄργανον) = instrument, tool; bodily organ

ornis, ornithos (ὄρνις) = bird

orthos (ὀρθός) = straight; right

osteon (ὀστέον) = bone

ostrakon (ὄστρακον) = tile

ous, otos (οὖς) = ear

P (π, φ, or ψ)

pachys (παχύς) = thick

paean (παιάν) = a song of thanksgiving to Apollo, the god of healing

paedia (παιδεία) = education

paes, paedos (παῖς) = child

paleos (παλαιός) = old

pan, pantos (πᾶν) = all

pancreas (πάγχρεας) = sweetbread (literally, all flesh)

papyros (πάπυρος) = the Egyptian papyrus plant

para (παρά) = beside, beyond, contrary to; irregular

paradigma (παράδειγμα) = pattern

pascho (πάσχω) = suffer, endure

pater (πατήρ) = father

pathos (πάθος) = feeling, sensation

pemptos (πέμπτος) = fifth

pente (πέντε) = five

pepto (πέπτω) = soften; cook; digest

peri (περί) = about, around, near

petros (πέτρος) = rock

phagein (φαγεῖν) = eat

phalanx (φάλαγξ) = body of soldiers

pharynx (φάρυγξ) = throat

pheno (φαίνω) = seem, appear; shine; pheno- (learned borrowing) = shining

phenomenon (φαινόμενον) = a thing come to light; appearance

phero (φέρω) = carry, bear

phileo (φιλέω) = to love

philia (φιλία) = love

phlegma (φλέγμα) = phlegm

phleps, phlebos (φλέψ, φλεβός) = artery

phobos (φόβος) = fear

phone (φονή) = sound

phos, photos (φῶς) = light

phren (φρήν) = partition or midriff

phyllon (φύλλον) = leaf

physis (φύσις) = nature

pithecos (πίθηκος) = ape

planao (πλανάω) = wander

planetes (πλανήτης) = wanderer, planet

plasticos (πλαστικός) = molded, formed

platys (πλατύς) = broad

plege (πληγή) = blow

pleura (πλευρά) = side; rib

pneo (πνέω) = breathe

pneumon (πνεύμων) = lung

poietes (ποιητής) = maker, poet

polemos (πόλεμος) = war

polis (πόλις) = city

poly (πολύ) = much, many

pous, podos (πούς) = foot

pragma (πρᾶγμα) = thing, deed

pro (πρό) = in front of

pros (πρός) = to, toward, in addition to

protos (πρῶτος) = first

pseudos (ψεῦδος) = false

psyche (ψυχή) = soul

pteron (πτερόν) = wing

pyloros (πυλωρός) = gatekeeper

pyr, pyros (πῦρ) = fire

R (ρ)

rheo (ῥέω) = flow

rhetor (ῥήτωρ) = speaker

rhis, rhinos (ῥίς) = nose

S (σ)

sacchar (σάκχαρ) = sugar

sarx, sarcos (σάρξ, σαρκός) = flesh

sauros (σαῦρος) = lizard

scene (σκηνή) = tent; stage backdrop

schema (σχῆμα) = form, shape, figure

schole (σχολή) = leisure

scleros (σκληρός) = hard

scopeo (σκοπέω) = look at

sideros (σίδηρος) = iron

skeletos (σκελετός) = dried up

soma, somatos (σῶμα) = body

sophia (σοφία) = wisdom

sophistes (σοφιστής) = expert, teacher

sophos (σοφός) = wise, clever

sphaera (σφαῖρα) = ball

sphongos (σφόγγος) = sponge

stadion (στάδιον) = race-course

stereos (στερεός) = solid, firm

sthenos (σθένος) = strength

stoa (στοά) = cloister, colonnade
stoma, stomatos (στόμα) = opening
strategos (στράτηγος) = general
symposion (συμπόσιον) = drinking party
syn (σύν) = with, together with
systema (σύστημα) = the whole; composition

T (τ or θ)

tachys (ταχύς) = fast
tauros (ταῦρος) = bull
techne (τέχνη) = skill, art
tele (τῆλε) = at a distance, far off
tessara (τέσσαρα) = four
tetartos (τέταρτος) = fourth
thanatos (θάνατος) = death
theao (θεάω) = look at, see
theatron (θέατρον) = theatre
theoria (θεωρία) = spectacle; contemplation
theos (θεός) = god
therapia (θεραπεία) = service
thermos (θερμός) = warm
thesauros (θησαυρός) = treasury

thrix, trichos (θρίξ, τριχός) = hair
tithemi (τίθημι) = put, place
tomos (τόμος) = cut
topos (τόπος) = place
trachea (τραχεῖα) = rough
tragoedia (τραγωδία) = tragedy; (literally, goat-song)
trauma (τραῦμα) = wound
treis (τρεῖς) = three
tris (τρίς) = three times
tritos (τρίτος) = third
trophe (τροφή) = food; nourishment
tympanon (τύμπανον) = drum
tyrannos (τύραννος) = absolute ruler

X (ξ)

xenos (ξένος) = stranger
xeros (ξηρός) = dry
xylon (ξύλον) = wood

Z (ζ)

zoon (ζῷον) = living thing
zyme (ζύμη) = leaven; yeast

NOTES